THE DIRTY, LAZY, KETO®

100 Easy Recipes Ready in under 30 Minutes

NO TIME TO COOK COOKBOOK

THE DIRTY LAZY KETO®

100 Easy Recipes Ready in under 30 Minutes

NO TIME TO COOK COOKBOOK

Stephanie Laska, MEd, and William Laska

ADAMS MEDIA

New York   London   Toronto   Sydney   New Delhi

Adams Media
An Imprint of Simon & Schuster, Inc.
100 Technology Center Drive
Stoughton, MA 02072

First Adams Media trade paperback edition January 2021

ADAMS MEDIA and colophon are trademarks of Simon & Schuster.

For information about special discounts for bulk purchases, please contact Simon & Schuster Special Sales at 1-866-506-1949 or business@simonandschuster.com.

The Simon & Schuster Speakers Bureau can bring authors to your live event. For more information or to book an event contact the Simon & Schuster Speakers Bureau at 1-866-248-3049 or visit our website at www.simonspeakers.com.

Interior design by Colleen Cunningham
Interior photographs by James Stefiuk
Interior images © Getty Images/maglyvi, nadyaillyustrator, Serhii Sereda, Nadzeya_Dzivakova, petite_lili, LanaMay; 123RF/sudowoodo, macrovector, Aksana Chubis, Mikalai Manyshau
Author photos by Stephanie Laska

Manufactured in the United States of America

4 2022

Library of Congress Cataloging-in-Publication Data
Names: Laska, Stephanie, author. | Laska, William, author.
Title: The DIRTY, LAZY, KETO® no time to cook cookbook / Stephanie Laska, MEd, William Laska.
Description: Avon, Massachusetts: Adams Media, 2021. | Series: DIRTY, LAZY, KETO® | Includes bibliographical references and index.
Identifiers: LCCN 2020034709 | ISBN 9781507214275 (pb) | ISBN 9781507214282 (ebook)
Subjects: LCSH: Reducing diets. | Ketogenic diet. | Quick and easy cooking. | LCGFT: Cookbooks.
Classification: LCC RM237.73 .L374 2021 | DDC 641.5/12--dc23
LC record available at https://lccn.loc.gov/2020034709

ISBN 978-1-5072-1427-5
ISBN 978-1-5072-1428-2 (ebook)

DEDICATION

I keep a box under my desk filled with letters from readers. I look at them again and again (especially in the wee hours when I'm writing). I feel comforted knowing that I'm not alone in struggling with my weight. For many of us, fighting obesity has been the biggest challenge of our lives.

The letters (okay, emails) come from all over the world, but they share the same themes—Hope. Relief. Inspiration!

> The success stories are far and wide. Readers are losing weight and reversing chronic health conditions with DIRTY, LAZY, KETO. *This is exciting.* We're onto something here, folks. Something big.

The secret is out and it's working. You can have your sugar-free cake and eat it too! It turns out *you don't have to be perfect to be successful.*

To all the weight loss rebels out there, this book is for you.

—Stephanie (*140 pounds, 8 years and counting!*)

In this book you'll find DIRTY, LAZY, KETO easy and economical recipes that still taste AMAZING. Join my family in the DLK kitchen, and let's do this together!

Special thanks to my social media advisors and liveliest recipe testers, Charlotte and Alex. Thank you for your patience and understanding while Mom and Dad embark on this keto journey to spread the word of this unbelievable way of eating that has such profound potential to change and save lives.

—#KetoOn! Bill

CONTENTS

To discover what these recipe icons mean, turn to page 18.

10. MAIN DISHES

11. DRINKS AND DESSERTS

PREFACE

A decade ago, if you would've told me I'd be publishing a *third* cookbook (about weight loss, nonetheless!), I would've thrown my head back and roared with laughter.

"Preposterous!" I would've yelled, shaking one fist in the air (while the other hand clutched a cold can of full-sugar Mountain Dew). That would've been the most outrageous prediction—*on so Many Levels*.

You see, I've always struggled with my weight.

> From second grade to my second marriage, I tended to weigh more than anyone else in the room.

I never had the time (or so I believed) to address the problem. After all, I was a busy mom of two—and working full-time. My schedule didn't have room for spending all day in the kitchen cooking fancy meals. I was more like a drive-thru or microwave type of girl, if we're being completely honest!

It's not like I could blame my weight on having kids. I gained more weight *after*, not during, my two pregnancies. It wasn't that I *wanted* to be morbidly obese. I just didn't know what to do about it. I weighed close to 300 pounds and felt stuck.

I stumbled into this way of eating, quite literally. I had just finished drinking a beer (or maybe two) at a friend's barbecue when I ran smack into her husband. I barely recognized him; he had lost so much weight! I was honestly surprised. You can guess what happened next. I quickly pulled him aside and whispered.

"*HOW* did you do it?"

His response was short and sweet. The secret to his losing forty pounds was eating only grilled chicken (while still drinking beer). Hmmm... *That's not at all what I expected.*

His menu recommendation didn't solve my weight problem (that's for sure). But ironically, I did walk away from that conversation feeling just a teensy, tiny bit inspired (and maybe a little buzzed). He made it sound so easy. Perhaps I too could take another crack at this whole dieting business. Maybe...*just maybe*...I would try to lose weight *one more time.*

That chance conversation, my friends, was the spark of inspiration that led me to create DIRTY, LAZY, KETO. With a lot of experimentation, I figured out that a matrix of higher-fat, moderate-protein, and lower-carb foods would help me to lose roughly ten pounds a month for a year and a half straight. Now don't get mad when I tell you this, but it wasn't that hard. I wasn't slaving over a hot stove all day. I didn't meander around a farmers' market smelling and squeezing produce (that's just weird). Rather, I learned to quickly shop for ingredients at "normal people" stores *and make healthy meals fast!*

> Here's the clincher though, folks: To achieve weight loss success, I finally realized I couldn't follow anyone else's rules about dieting. I had to do it in my own way.

I ended up losing 140 pounds total, or about half of my entire body weight. I've kept that amount of weight off for eight years now. *Eight!* (That's the equivalent of, like, 800 in dieting years.) With this kind of track record, it seems I've conquered the impossible. Ironically, I've managed to do this without changing the amount of time I spend in the kitchen. I'm still a busy working mom. That part didn't change!

I don't plan on keeping my methods a secret. I feel passionately that I'm onto something really big here. My mission is to fight obesity, not just at my house, but at your house too. I won't shut up about DIRTY, LAZY, KETO. In fact, it's pretty much all I talk about!

Folks new to DIRTY, LAZY, KETO usually start off by asking me one question:

"What do you eat?"

The conversation quickly morphs, however, into a deep discussion about much more than food. Losing weight isn't an exact science. You can't just eliminate carbs, "say no to bread," and become skinny overnight. It doesn't happen that way (unfortunately!). Making meaningful changes is a much more complicated process.

> DIRTY, LAZY, KETO isn't a temporary quick fix;
> it's a lifestyle.

My books and support groups have helped literally hundreds of thousands of people to lose weight *just like I did*. **My method works!**

To get started on your weight loss journey, you'll need an experienced guide. There's no time to waste. I'm going to be that person for you. Trust me to help you, and I'll show you the way.

We will do this together, my friend. Let's fight one carb at a time and make meals in 30 minutes or less. You CAN do this.

#KetoOn!

Stephanie

INTRODUCTION

No time to cook? *No problem!* Put down the takeout menus—I'm here to help.

I lost 140 pounds and have kept the weight off for eight years by taking shortcuts in the kitchen. I live by the mantra "You don't have to be perfect to be successful." I may not be a professionally trained chef, but I sure am an experienced eater!

I created DIRTY, LAZY, KETO when I was working full-time while managing a hectic household. At the end of a busy day, I had to get dinner on the table—*fast!* There was no time to waste preparing unnecessary ingredients, or worse, making a meal my family wouldn't like. Instead, I got to work creating quick-fix DIRTY, LAZY, KETO meals that would help me to lose weight while being delicious enough for my whole family to enjoy (even my picky eaters!).

With lots of humor and practical tips, I'm here to share my fast and favorite family recipes. Inside *The DIRTY, LAZY, KETO® No Time to Cook Cookbook*, you'll find 100 great-tasting recipes—all 10 grams net carbs or less—that you can make in 30 minutes or less. *That's including prep time, people!* As always, the ingredients can even be found at discount grocery stores—nothing fancy required. That's just not how I roll. With simple, stress-free instructions, you'll have dinner ready and on the table before a delivery guy could possibly arrive at your doorstep.

Each dish is created from the DIRTY, LAZY, KETO basics: healthy fats, lean protein, and slow-burning carbs. You'll find:

- Recipes that can be prepared in under 30 minutes, including prep time!
- Helpful shortcuts for food prep and execution
- Suggestions to add variety or adjust the recipe to your tastes
- Macronutrients in line with DIRTY, LAZY, KETO principles
- Recipes that are no more than 10 grams net carbs per serving
- Tasty, time-saving "remixes" that transform yesterday's leftovers into an entirely new meal or snack to enjoy today
- One pot/one bowl recipes that save you tons of cleanup time

The *DIRTY, LAZY, KETO® No Time to Cook Cookbook* has everyone covered—from meals for picky eaters or big eaters, to fancier meals for guests and vegetarian-"ish" options (that don't contain meat, but may contain dairy or eggs). I designate how recipes meet a variety of needs by assigning these handy-dandy icons throughout the cookbook:

 REBOOT: It's a *"twofer"*! Make extra and use part for another meal.

 LESS MESS: One pot—one bowl? *Minimal* dish-washing.

 I'M HANGRY! Big-eater meals to *fill you up*!

 PICKY EATERS? *He likes it! She likes it!* Crowd-pleasing favorites.

 FANCY ENOUGH FOR GUESTS: *Ooh la la...* Looks impressive and tastes great!

 VEGETARIAN-"ISH": *"Kinda"* meatless, but may still call for dairy and/or eggs.

DIRTY, LAZY, KETO is a flexible, honest, real-world approach to losing weight while still living a normal life.

You'll find shortcuts throughout this cookbook to save you time and help you get food on the table in 30 minutes or less. Losing weight doesn't have to be complicated or time-consuming!

The *DIRTY, LAZY, KETO® No Time to Cook Cookbook* empowers you to keto your own way—in a style and on a schedule that works for *you*. Recipes in this judgment-free cookbook support your unique path to sustainable weight loss, *not perfection*.

Let's get started!

DIRTY, LAZY, KETO

SHORTCUTS

No Time? No Problem!

CHAPTER 1

DIRTY, LAZY, KETO CHECK-IN

KEEP IT REAL—START WHERE YOU'RE AT

Growing up, my husband and I both ate the same rotation of
meals for dinner. Even though we lived a world apart, our families
were equally *uncreative* in the kitchen (sorry, Mom!). We ate a
similar conga line of basic American meals: spaghetti, hamburgers,
tacos, lasagna, meat and potatoes, and, let's not forget, *leftovers*.
Neither of us were exposed to any kind of fancy cooking; if we
were experts at anything, it was *eating*.

Even without formal training, everyone knows what good food
tastes like. That is all that matters when you're learning how to
cook. Why spend time making food if you don't like the end
result? The meal has to be worth your while. At the same time,
most people don't want to spend an arm and a leg on ingredients
or be chained to a stove all day long. There has to be a balance.

> DIRTY, LAZY, KETO recipes aren't complicated,
> time-consuming, or expensive.

You don't need to take out a second mortgage to buy ingredients or
take the afternoon off work to figure out what to do. The stress of
cooking healthier shouldn't cause you to bow out and sign up for a
meal delivery service. You can do this on your own! No matter what
your comfort level is in the kitchen, I'm going to help you get in and
out of the kitchen fast—*one DIRTY, LAZY, KETO meal at a time.*

I lost 140 pounds and have maintained my weight loss for eight years by making recipes like these. The meals, snacks, and desserts are easy to make, and just as important, taste fantastic.

> I'm not missing out on "old favorites" because I am still enjoying them—I can make a modified low-carb version of just about anything!

Unlike other strict diets, DIRTY, LAZY, KETO is a complete lifestyle that you can follow forever. It's flexible, practical, and sustainable for the long haul. I'm living proof!

WHAT IS DIRTY, LAZY, KETO?

In my world, Dirty Keto means anything goes. No foods are "off the table" as long as you stay within your daily target amount of net carbs. If you want to eat a hot dog for lunch or drink a Diet Coke with dinner, then I say *do it*. Who am I to judge? Personally, I enjoyed many of these *so-called* "taboo" foods and I still lost weight. It's your choice whether or not to eat "Dirty Keto" foods like low-carb tortillas, shredded cheese, lunch meat, alcohol, sugar-free candy, low-carb ice cream, or zero-carb energy drinks. Only you can make that call. I won't judge your lifestyle for even a second.

Only you get to decide what to eat. Go ahead and show the keto police the door. Their criticism is not welcome here. *Buh-bye!*

To lose weight with DIRTY, LAZY, KETO, you don't have to follow rigid macronutrient guidelines. Lazy Keto is just as effective as the Strict Keto diet. Maybe even more so! You don't have to count calories, fat grams, amounts of protein, *and* net carbs to be successful with weight loss. **Lazy Keto means only tracking net carbs.** That was my strategy, and I found it extremely effective; I've helped thousands of others to do the same.

If my way sounds too loosey-goosey to be effective with your personality type, that's okay too. Some people find that strict counting of macronutrients helps them be more accountable. It's important that you follow your instincts. You can be strict with counting and "dirty" with ingredient choices if that tickles your fancy. DIRTY, LAZY, KETO supports you either way. In fact, here in this cookbook, I provide expanded nutrition information for every recipe. You will find accurate net carb counts per serving as well as the number of calories, and grams of fat, protein, sodium, fiber, carbohydrates, and sugar.

All methods are welcome here. Have a seat and get comfortable.

If the mere mention of doing complicated math causes your blood pressure to skyrocket, however, let me provide you with some reassurance. *You are not alone!* I can't handle advanced math problems either. I lost my weight without ever counting a single calorie, protein gram, or fat gram. I didn't use an app, nor did I make graphs or charts; I only kept track of net carbs. I ate 20–50 grams of net carbs per day. That's it! *I consistently lost weight.* That's Lazy Keto in a nutshell, folks.* I could talk about this all day long—no other topic gets me this excited!

> DIRTY, LAZY, KETO is so simple, yet it works.

Before we start cooking, let's review a couple of basics, including how to calculate net carbs, the DLK food pyramid, foods to avoid, and approved drinks.We need to level-set our knowledge so everyone is on the same page.

First, you'll need to identify the key markers of a nutrition label with DIRTY, LAZY, KETO. Let's get started.

1. Notice the serving size.
2. Find the Total Carbohydrate number.
3. Subtract the amount of Dietary Fiber.
4. Subtract the amount of Sugar Alcohols (if applicable).
5. The result is the NET CARBS per serving.

Here's an example:

Nutrition Facts

Serving Size 1/2 Cup (64g)
Servings Per Container 4

Amount Per Serving

Calories 80	Calories from Fat 25
	% Daily Value*
Total Fat 2.5g	**4%**
Saturated Fat 1.5g	**8%**
Trans Fat 0g	
Cholesterol 45mg	**15%**
Sodium 110mg	**5%**
Total Carbohydrate 13g	**4%**
Dietary Fiber 2g	**8%**
Sugars 6g	
Sugar Alcohol 5g	
Protein 5g	**10%**
Vitamin A 2%	Vitamin C 0%
Calcium 10%	Iron 2%
*Percent Daily Values are based on a 2,000 calorie diet.	

13
−2
−5
⃝6

I wish I could tell you the magic number of net carbs you'll need to eat to ensure weight loss, but I believe that number is different for everyone. Age, activity level, hormones, and gender affect our metabolism.

| **TIER 1** | **FRUITS, NUTS, AND SEEDS** | EAT JUST A HANDFUL |

| **TIER 2** | **FULL-FAT DAIRY** | LIMIT—USE COMMON SENSE |

| **TIER 3** | **NIGHTSHADE VEGETABLES** | EAT WITH CAUTION |

| **TIER 4** | **NONSTARCHY VEGETABLES, HEALTHY FATS, LEAN PROTEINS** | WILL HELP KEEP YOU FULL |

TIPS

Eat lots of nonstarchy vegetables!
Eat fats with your vegetables to make them more enjoyable.
Use fat only for satiety and satisfaction, not as a goal or as a food group.

AVOID

| Bread | Pasta | Sugar | Milk | Corn | Beans | Rice |

| Water | Diet Soda | Tea | Coffee | Dry Wine | Spirits |

To help explain why DIRTY, LAZY, KETO is so effective, I wrote a full support guide, *DIRTY, LAZY, KETO*®: *Get Started Losing Weight While Breaking the Rules* (St. Martin's Essentials, 2020). In this DLK handbook, I go into detail about how to start and make recommendations for what to eat. I give you the framework for success, but with helpful girlfriend advice to consider when things get rough. After all, we know food is just one part of the weight loss riddle!

WHAT'S REALLY STOPPING YOU?

Who's ready to start cooking? Are you PUMPED UP? Wait a minute… Why isn't anyone raising their hand?

You have a cookbook in front of you, but I notice you haven't started cooking yet. What are you waiting for?! Okay, *okay*…instead of harassing you, let me try a more empathetic approach. I might be able to guess why you're procrastinating. If you haven't cooked in a while (or ever!), you may be feeling a bit lost or intimidated. Those are valid feelings. It can be scary to try new things. Is that all, though?

Sometimes we tell ourselves little fibs to stall for time. If that describes your situation, let me help pull the wool away from your eyes. Let's evaluate and debunk common myths about cooking that may be blocking your culinary progress.

I'm Not a Good Cook

To get you over the hump, let's redefine *cooking* to mean "fixing." Good cooks don't have to be gourmets; they just have to follow directions. I make DIRTY, LAZY, KETO recipes doable for everyone. Using easy-to-follow terms, I'll walk you through the exact steps needed to make one hundred scrumptious recipes. I promise to "keep it real" at all times. Strategies I use in *The DIRTY, LAZY, KETO® No Time to Cook Cookbook* are:

- Keep directions simple (not elaborate)
- Assemble already prepared ingredients (as opposed to making them from scratch)
- Take shortcuts (no wasting time)
- Simple execution (avoid unnecessary steps)

I'm Too Tired to Cook

It can be challenging to lose weight if you are constantly eating restaurant food. Portion control, limited menu choices, questionable ingredients, and social pressure all contribute to weight loss mayhem. *That's just not going to work!*

Additionally, many people mistake ordering takeout or eating meals at restaurants for bona fide "rewards" when they feel tired.

"I've worked a long day; I deserve to go out to eat."

Does that sound familiar?

> Food is not a treat (unless you are a dog). Instead, substitute healthier ways to reward yourself by *making more time for you.*

I Don't Know How to Cook

Start where you're at. No one is judging you! Set small, realistic goals. In fact, I recommend you aim *as low as possible* (don't laugh!). I use this technique often when trying to build up my confidence. By setting the bar low, I find it easier to become an overachiever. For instance, you could set a goal to make one meal per week from the cookbook. That sounds easy enough, right?

By expecting progress (not perfection) from yourself, you are much more likely to succeed. Interestingly, the pride and confidence that grow from learning a new skill (like cooking) will spill into other areas of your weight loss journey. Today, you conquer roasting a chicken, but tomorrow, *the world*!

Cooking Is Expensive

DIRTY, LAZY, KETO recipes are more affordable than going out to eat (for any ultra-cheapskates out there, you'll have fun poking around our last book, *The DIRTY, LAZY, KETO® Dirt Cheap Cookbook*). Every ingredient called for here is most likely something you're already familiar with. You probably have it in your kitchen right now! *Nothing fancy or expensive is required here.* Ingredients are available at your local grocery store.

Aside from your grocery bill, think about the money you'll save in the long run by losing weight. Healthier people don't get sick as often. Your overall quality of life will improve. *How much is that worth to you?*

I'll Have to Make Separate Meals

Everyone in your family can enjoy the same meal. DIRTY, LAZY, KETO recipes taste so decadent and delicious that folks will likely become suspicious about how these will help you lose weight! To help meet the needs of varying tastes, though, I provide suggested tips and tricks throughout the cookbook for you to make desired modifications. Recipes are designated with convenient "callouts" for specific audiences too. At the top of each recipe, symbols are used to inform you when a dish is perfect for picky eaters, guests coming over for dinner, those feeling extra hungry, and even those wanting something vegetarian-"ish" (no meat but may contain dairy/eggs).

I Have No Time

We all lead busy lives. At first glance, your packed schedule might seem too full for home cooking. I understand. But what happens when you take a closer look? Sometimes freeing up a window of time to cook is as simple as moving routines around or delegating tasks to others.

If that's not the case, though, and you're still pushing back about not having any free time, I suggest you have a more honest conversation with yourself. Is it possible your day is overscheduled on purpose? As a form of procrastination, many of us put personal needs last on the list. This is a sneaky way to avoid taking action.

> Prioritizing your health is a decision that only you can make.

Once you commit, however, I'll be there to help you the rest of the way. (I promise it won't take all day either.) *The DIRTY, LAZY, KETO® No Time to Cook Cookbook* gives you all the immediate tools necessary to make healthy meals—and *fast*! I'll help you deliver results in 30 minutes or less.

DLK PEP TALK

I'm sensing you're finally ready to get started. This is going to be quite the adventure. Roll up your sleeves, my friend, because it's time to get down and dirty in the kitchen! (Don't worry, I'll give you tips for cleanup too.) With *The DIRTY, LAZY, KETO® No Time to Cook Cookbook* in hand, you'll learn how to prep your kitchen for maximum efficiency and execute meals at lightning speed. I'll be coaching you with specifics from the sidelines. As an added bonus, I promise to tell entertaining and encouraging stories every step of the way.

CHAPTER 2

GET READY FOR ACTION!

SET THE STAGE FOR SPEED

Organization is the name of the game for fast cooking. You need the right tools, sure, but more important, you need them at your fingertips. The 30-minute clock is ticking and we can't waste time looking for something.

Before you even think of preheating the oven, it's time to tidy up. You're going to need space to work, after all. I don't know about you, but my kitchen island is like a magnet for everything *unrelated* to cooking. Mail, homework, art projects, and dog leashes keep showing up, *no matter how many times I put them away*. It's maddening! In order to have a functioning kitchen, though, you have to stake your claim on the kitchen real estate and keep out trespassers.

> Removing unnecessary clutter from countertops is imperative for speedy cooking.

Now that you have cleared a space to work, you're going to cover the counters with all of your kitchen gadgets, cookware, and packaged food from your pantry. Yes, get *everything* out! Crawl under cabinets, empty the drawers, and unpack every shelf. Keep going! Don't stop until the cupboards are bare. Yes, we're getting all Marie Kondo in your kitchen, but we'll be doing it *DIRTY, LAZY, KETO style*.

A surprising reward for completing this activity is the likelihood of finding hidden treasures. Like the missing sock vortex in the laundry room, every kitchen has a black hole of forgotten items. Who knows what you might find? When cleaning out my own cabinets, I found a partially wrapped air fryer from last Christmas. *Score!* You might discover items you assumed were lost, or even better, stumble upon sentimental heirlooms. I know you'll find at least one surprise. *Press on.*

DO THE THREE-STEP SHUFFLE

Once you see everything you own, it's time to **analyze, evaluate, and organize**. Start by grouping similar items together—appliances in one spot, canned goods in another, for example. Did you discover anything obvious to get rid of? Getting rid of damaged equipment, duplicate items, or expired food is an easy place to start. Determining what *else* to get rid of, though? Well, that can be tricky.

As you evaluate what's spread out on the countertops, think about the current needs of your household. Ask yourself guiding questions to help you decide what stays and what goes: *How often is this used? Do I throw big parties? How many people do I serve at once? Does this have important sentimental value?*

Step 1. Let It Go!

Once you make a decision to get rid of something, remove it immediately. Load donations right away into the trunk of your car and fill the trash can with the rest.

- To charity—donate duplicate kitchen tools, junk food, items you don't use or no longer need.
- To the trash—send expired food, and broken or damaged equipment.

Step 2. Make It "Purty"

Clean the bare shelves and cabinets. How often are they empty like this, after all? Cleaning the space can be as simple or as elaborate as you'd like. At the very least, use the extension arm on your vacuum to suck out floating dust bunnies and spills from spices. If you have more energy, consider lining the shelves. Take note of anything that needs repairing, like broken hinges or knobs. The goal here is to maximize your available space; make sure every bit of storage space can be utilized.

Step 3. Create Workstations

Before you start shoving items back into your (now clean!) cabinets, I'm going to challenge you to have an open mind and consider a new organizational system. Instead of putting things back in the same place they've always been, let's do something different.

> Organize tools by their intended purpose and in a cabinet/drawer closest to where they will be used.

This strategy eliminates time searching for what you need. You'll have what you need and where you'll need it from the get-go. This method saves oodles of time!

Don't worry, I'll provide suggestions for how to organize your space. Not all of my ideas will apply (or appeal to your household). *That's okay!* Not everyone drinks coffee or has an outdoor grill; my suggestions aren't mandatory. I encourage you to create workstations based on your unique family needs. Be creative!

Before we begin, let me share a few caveats. Don't stress if you don't have the items I describe. They aren't necessarily required. I'm only trying to help you organize what you may have on hand. Later, I will provide a list of "must-have" items. *Stay tuned!* Second, don't be surprised that items often overlap. Expect intentional duplicates (when appropriate) in your workstations. I keep packages of sugar-free sweetener in two stations—my coffee area and my baking station. I store aluminum foil in *both* my grilling section *and* food packing drawer. The convenience of having the exact item where it's needed is worth the expense and trouble of stocking the same item in two places.

With efficiency in mind, carefully select the most appropriate spot for each station. You know your kitchen better than anyone else. How can you best use your space?

VEGETABLE PREP AREA
Choose a location nearest the sink to house cutting boards, colanders, and related kitchen tools (sharp knives, peeler, and so on). If

you don't have a kitchen drawer or cupboard for utensils next to your sink, think outside the box—place the items in a decorative cup instead (be careful with knives—safety first!).

BAKING SECTION

Gather all currently owned baking ingredients and cookware to store in one spot. Unless you bake often, the baking section could be off the beaten path in your kitchen. Baking hardware found in this section might be a mixer, mixing bowl, muffin tin, whisk, spring pan, nonstick baking sheet, Pyrex baking dish, measuring cups, measuring spoons, and so on. Common baking ingredients also stored here include coconut flour, almond flour, baking soda, baking powder, artificial sweetener, unsweetened coconut, 100% cocoa powder, and nonstick cooking spray.

MAIN MEAL STATION

Stow essential dinner-making tools next to the cooking area (stove-top, oven, and microwave). Examples include pots, pans, skillets, and specialty cooking trays (like a pizza pan). Helpful gadgets to stash in this section include a can opener, spatula, tongs, measuring cups, measuring spoons, pizza cutter, rubber spatula, oven mitts, and meat thermometer. Include food items here too, like cooking oils and spices.

FOOD PACKING

Organize available food storage containers (but only with match-ing lids!) to improve efficiency. In the same spot, keep a supply of disposables (aluminum foil, parchment paper, Ziploc bags, plastic wrap, and so on). Twist ties, lunch sacks, and permanent markers are helpful too.

KITCHEN APPLIANCE STORAGE

Shelve practical appliances you love (and know how to use!) along-side their ancillary parts in one centralized location (waffle maker, pressure cooker, slow cooker, blender, mixer, food processor, elec-tric wok, and air fryer).

Instead of crawling on my hands and knees on the floor of the kitchen trying to find a particular kitchen appliance (and its accessories!), I finally had the bright idea to move them all to one spot, *out in the open*. I have my kitchen appliances lined up on a stainless steel rack next to my kitchen table. Yes, this shelf is a bit of an eyesore, I'll admit. But the time I've saved by being able to grab what I need? *It's so worth it.*

COFFEE AND TEA CART
Store coffee- and tea-related items adjacent to your coffee maker or teapot (mugs, ground coffee, immersion blender, filters, stir sticks, artificial sweetener packets, flavored sugar-free syrups, tea bags, and so on).

OUTDOOR GRILLING
Secure outdoor cooking–related items in one location. These include barbecue tools, an apron, long matches, outdoor foil, oven mitts, and so on.

PARTY SUPPLIES
Pack rarely used items (disposable party napkins, themed paper plates, birthday candles, holiday platters, tablecloths, travel potluck containers, etc.) out of the way, *relocated out of the kitchen altogether* if you have the space. I keep party decorations in my hall closet, and party platters and travel food containers are in my garage.

EATING STATION
In the space closest to the dishwasher (and the area where you eat meals), stack serving plates, silverware, and glasses, in addition to disposable plates, napkins, and cups.

CLEANUP SUPPLIES
Keep cleaning products (trash bags, antibacterial soap, dish soap, dishwasher soap, pot scrubber, antibacterial wipes, bleach spray, paper towels, and so on) stocked and accessible to help maintain a healthy and clean cooking environment.

FILL IN THE GAPS

Now that you have a better understanding of what's available in your kitchen, you can get to work filling in any gaps. Remove any potential barriers in your path to fast cooking. If you need a pressure cooker to make cooking easier, then so be it!

> Having a fully functioning kitchen is an investment in your health.

Go ahead and make a list of the outstanding tools you need. Replacing broken, outdated, or missing kitchen items doesn't have to break the bank. You won't need to max out your credit card. Before heading to the mall, try stopping by a thrift store first. You might be surprised at the selection of donated kitchen tools and quality bakeware. You never know what treasure you'll find! Shopping at discount (or dollar) stores is another viable option, especially for smaller, inexpensive items. Lastly, don't be afraid to ask for help. Send an email to friends and family with your wish list or offer to do a trade.

> Upgrade your kitchen supplies over time; for now, just start with acquiring the basics.

STEPHANIE'S FAST COOKING ESSENTIALS

- **Tools and Gadgets:** colander, sharp knives, pizza cutter, julienne vegetable peeler, silicone spatula, kitchen shears, meat thermometer, immersion blender, whisk
- **Cookware:** nonstick baking sheet, skillet, pots/pans, glass Pyrex dishes, muffin tin, pizza pan
- **Appliances:** pressure cooker with accessories (steamer basket, muffin tin), slow cooker, blender, mixer, waffle maker, microwave, air fryer, food processor
- **Duplicates:** mixing bowls, measuring cups, measuring spoons, food storage containers, small dishwasher-safe cutting boards
- **Disposables:** Ziploc bags in all sizes, parchment paper, extra-large heavy-duty aluminum foil, aluminum foil sheets, heavy-duty plastic wrap

Now that your kitchen is efficiently prepared and organized to support speedy cooking, you're ready to tackle the next step: food!

CHAPTER 3

CLOCK'S TICKIN'—30 MINUTES OR LESS

SECRET SAUCE FOR FAST COOKING?

Finally! We're ready to talk about my favorite part—*food*! You'll quickly discover how important it is to buy the *right ingredients* at the store. By *right*, I mean "correctly packaged." Cauliflower is sold a dozen ways, for example, and the subtle nuances between each choice affect how much time is required for prepping and cooking (and net carb count too!). To help you avoid any potential pitfalls, I'll share my DIRTY, LAZY, KETO shopping hacks for selecting the perfect time-saving ingredients.

To start, you'll need to arm yourself with a strategic shopping list. You don't want to waste your precious time aimlessly meandering down every aisle looking for something that "looks good." An itemized list isn't the only thing you'll need. You must also bring a sharp and critical mind. Judiciously choose what ingredients to buy. Challenge every purchase decision.

"Will *this* help me cook fast?"

If the answer is no, *put that sucker back.*

Too often, we get caught up in the shopping experience. We become distracted by discounts or begin romanticizing what we're willing or capable of doing in the kitchen. In the produce aisle, a

BOGO cauliflower promotion tempts you to fill up your cart with a dozen heads. *It's on sale, right?* You might become delusional, thinking of spending the afternoon making organic riced cauliflower with a Cuisinart food processor (and you don't own one!). Slap both cheeks and wake up from that fantasy! I don't want you feeling bad when those dreams turn into a nightmare of moldy cauliflower.

You don't have to make ingredients from scratch to lose weight.

> Unlike other strict diets, DIRTY, LAZY, KETO empowers you to cheat with artificial ingredients and time-saving tricks in the kitchen.

Food doesn't have to be locally sourced, organic, or 100 percent homemade for you to lose weight. Let me assure you that it's okay to cut corners! I lost 140 pounds by using tricks like these on a regular basis. Stop trying to be Martha Stewart already and *just be you.* Embrace these dirty or lazy tips and free yourself from judgment.

TAKE INGREDIENT SHORTCUTS

At the store, I shop for ingredients that help make cooking fast. *Do they cost more?* Sometimes, yes, but not always. There are plenty of ways to buy shortcut ingredients at discounted prices. When I stumble upon a good sale, I take advantage and buy extra. My pantry and freezer are chock-full. I'm also flexible with meal planning. I've been known to spontaneously change my dinner plans after discovering a tempting sale. Occasionally, when it's important to me, I choose to spend more money when I know it will save me time later. Ingredient shortcuts to consider:

- **Precooked Meats.** Rotisserie chicken, cooked shrimp, and precooked sausage make meal assembly a snap. Check the inventory of your grocery store deli and you might discover a wide variety of precooked meats at competitive prices.
- **Prewashed, Precut Veggies**. Speed up meal prep by taking produce shortcuts. Buy shredded coleslaw, bags of prewashed spinach, or freshly cleaned and sliced mushrooms and bypass meal prep. I even buy jars of preminced garlic to skip a step while cooking.

- **Frozen Foods.** Fresh is not always the best choice when it comes to speedy cooking. Vegetables like riced cauliflower, zoodles, or fajita mix can transform a meal in seconds—*straight from the freezer!* May I remind you that frozen berries don't need washing? Flash-frozen (individually portioned) meats also save time without ever sacrificing flavor.
- **Premade Sauces.** Stock your pantry or fridge with assorted sauce starters: Alfredo sauce, no-sugar-added marinara sauce, or Indian simmer sauces.
- **Jarred or Canned Items.** With virtually no prep time needed, canned foods reduce cook time. I sometimes prefer the flavor of canned versus fresh. Examples of my favorites include canned green beans, artichoke hearts, and coconut milk.
- **Direct-to-Microwave Vegetables.** More and more vegetables are being sold in microwave-ready packages. You don't even have to stab the package with a fork to vent the bag before heating! (Can you get lazier than that?) So far, I've discovered Brussels sprouts, green beans, riced cauliflower, and broccoli florets sold in these miraculous, time-saving pouches.

MENTALLY PREPARING

Having the right ingredients on hand is only half the battle when it comes to speed cooking. What you do with them next is equally important. To make recipes in 30 minutes or less, you'll need to apply time-saving strategies in the kitchen *at every step.* For me, this starts with meal planning.

Hunt and Gather

Before I go to bed at night, I think about what I'll eat the next day (don't judge). I spend a few minutes in the kitchen looking for needed ingredients, making notes of any missing items on a shopping list. I pull required items from the pantry and glance at the spice rack to make sure I have everything I need. In one messy pile, I dump the ingredients onto the kitchen counter. Depending on what I'm making, I'll drag out necessary cooking gadgets (like a slow cooker) and add it to the heap. Lastly, before I head to bed, I transfer frozen meat to the fridge to safely thaw.

When I wake up the next day, I have a smile on my face. I'm prepped for success! I've removed any anxiety or guesswork about what to eat for dinner. Sure, I might have to stop by the store for any missing ingredients (let's be realistic, this happens), but aside from any hiccups, I'm ready for action.

Before You Start

Cooking a meal goes much more smoothly when everything is ready from the get-go. Assemble all necessary ingredients in one spot before you start. Prep ingredients ahead of time with speed in mind.

- Start with thawed meat.
- Buy smaller cuts of meat to begin with (smaller pieces cook faster).
- Transform larger cuts of meat into smaller sizes (pound into thin slices, cut into smaller pieces or strips).
- Prep vegetables (wash, clean, cut) ahead of time.
- Chop food into smaller, evenly sized pieces (for even cooking time).
- Open every package at once.

FLASH COOKING METHODS

When it's time to actually cook the food, choose methods that speed up the process. You don't have to sacrifice flavor during this step. Think about ways you can bring the heat to get the job done in the most efficient way possible.

- **Be "Spacy."** Spread out food so it cooks efficiently and evenly, both horizontally and vertically. Strive for thin layers of food; thicker cuts require additional cook time.
- **Fat Is Your Friend.** Don't be afraid to use fats like oil when cooking. Remember, DIRTY, LAZY, KETO recommends using fat to make healthy food taste better! In addition to helping with satiety, fat helps food to cook faster.
- **Execute.** Turn up the heat! Use hot methods of cooking to get the job done quicker. While it might seem obvious, some methods of cooking are faster than others, including:
  - Outdoor grilling
  - Baking in the oven at higher temperatures

- Broiling food on high
- Stovetop cooking on medium to high heat
- **Go, Go, Gadget!** Don't be afraid to use plug-in gadgets to help you cook faster. Some might surprise you (like an air fryer)! Overall, gadgets speed up cooking by helping you to multitask. They also free up valuable stovetop space. Here are some that I find very helpful.
  - Pressure cooker
  - Air fryer
  - Electric wok
  - Waffle maker
- **Multitask.** Get more done (in less time) by doing several jobs at once. This doesn't have to be stressful. Multitasking can be as simple as precooking vegetables in the microwave while stir-frying meat on the stovetop. Don't be afraid to use unconventional cooking methods. Get creative and #breaktherules. For example:
  - Instead of cooking bacon in a frying pan, bake it in the oven.
  - Use a pressure cooker to make hard-boiled eggs.
  - Microwave scrambled eggs.
  - Use a waffle maker to grill sausage.

DOUBLE OR NOTHING

Think several steps ahead when prepping for a meal. If you're cleaning one stalk of celery, why not clean two? Better yet, prep all the vegetables for the week at once. As long as you're planning on using the food in the immediate future, doubling up on a job now saves time later. Additionally, I recommend you reboot entire portions of your meal from one day to the next. Call it leftovers or creative meal planning, but taking practical shortcuts like these saves valuable time.

- Make double portions of a meal and freeze the second one for later.
- Cook or chop double the amount of an ingredient to use again later in the week.
- Recycle leftovers from today's meal. Enjoy again tomorrow.

BE A TECHNO

Use hands-free available technology to help problem solve in the kitchen. You won't have to stop what you're doing to look something up.

"Alexa, how many tablespoons are in a cup?"

"Alexa, how do you make pesto?"

Pair cooking with music or listening to a podcast to make it more enjoyable.

"Alexa, play Italian cooking music on Spotify."

Set cooking timers and reminders with Siri and Alexa to keep yourself on schedule.

"Alexa, remind me to defrost steaks for dinner at six a.m. tomorrow."

"Siri, set a 10-minute bacon timer."

When you're not in the kitchen, plan ahead for what to make. Use your iPad or other digital device to search and store recipes. This is much faster than flipping through cookbooks (this cookbook excluded, of course!).

TIME TO EAT? BUT I'M NOT HUNGRY.

Stop making meals just because you feel like *you are supposed to.* If your family is too busy (or not interested) in eating a big dinner, then don't make one! Or maybe your family would prefer to sit down for lunch instead? Society's norms may not apply to you—*and that's just fine.* Not a morning eater? Skip breakfast, I say! By empowering yourself to follow your own rhythm, you'll eat DIRTY, LAZY, KETO foods when you actually feel hungry, not because it's "time." This strategy will save you crazy amounts of time (and frustration) in the kitchen.

Stop making meals no one wants to eat; #BreaktheRules! Eat breakfast for dinner, leftover dinner for lunch, or lunch foods for breakfast.

Do what works for you and your body, and do it on your own schedule.

CHAPTER 4

NO MESS COOKIN'

BE FAST, EFFICIENT, EFFECTIVE...AND FABULOUS

In my kitchen, we maintain order (and sanity!) by operating under one guiding principle: "Start clean, end clean." Yes, there might be some swear words yelled when the bacon burns—*language doesn't count*—but with everything else, we try our best to keep the kitchen tidy.

How does that work on a day-to-day basis? At my house, I expect the kitchen to look tidy *before* I even start cooking. Clean dishes from the dishwasher are put away, the sink is empty, and counters are cleared of distractions and interferences *before* I start making a meal. It's like a painter sitting down to create a masterpiece. He wants to start with fresh brushes and a blank canvas, right? If you're going to create a work of art in the kitchen, you too need a clean slate.

From a practical standpoint, I've had to break the "start clean, end clean" message down to specifics to avoid any confusion about what I'm asking for. Don't laugh, but sometimes folks need clear directions.

- You ate it? *You clean it up.* Walk your dishes back to the sink.
- Rinse your plate/cup/silverware after use and load directly into the dishwasher.
- Push food scraps down the disposal with running water until it magically disappears.

- Instead of complaining that the trash smells, take the bag out to the curb!
- When the milk carton is empty (or anything else in the fridge, for that matter), throw it away but add that item to the grocery list.

Your house rules may be different from mine. Everyone has different hot buttons. One of mine, for example, is the necessity to cover the food inside the microwave. It only takes a second for a nuclear-style explosion to occur. Using an inexpensive food cover or removable tray in the microwave is an insurance policy for easy cleanup, but it's only effective when people actually use it. Otherwise, mayhem occurs. No one ever admits to causing a marinara sauce detonation!

Maintaining order like this requires teamwork. Rather than leaving standards up to interpretation, I recommend being direct and blunt with your expectations (and maybe even LOUD!).

"Do you want dinner or *NOT*, people?"

You're not asking for much here, so stop feeling guilty. No one is doing *you* a favor by cleaning up after *themselves*. **Keeping the kitchen clean is about common decency and courteousness.** These are life skills needed for adulthood. Your family should be thanking you!

MINIMIZE MESS

Do yourself a favor. Do more with less *from the get-go*.

Intentionally streamlining your cooking methods will help you get in and out of the kitchen fast. I'll teach you how to make DIRTY, LAZY, KETO meals in 30 minutes or less, and in a way that reduces any unnecessary cleanup afterward.

My favorite "clean" cooking methods require a limited number of pots or pans. When you're finished cooking, there shouldn't be a pile of dirty pots and pans left behind in the sink.

ONE-STOP SHOP

- **Sheet Pan.** Line a 12" × 18" (or equivalent) baking sheet pan with extra-large aluminum foil or parchment paper and bake all of the ingredients you need at the same time. Clean up *in seconds* by simply throwing away the lining. *Hello!*
- **Disposables.** Use disposable aluminum trays for cooking or leave them behind at a potluck or barbecue for your host to reuse.

PIONEER MODE

- **Grill.** After you're finished cooking on the barbecue, crank up the heat *caveman-style* and burn off any remaining food that was stuck to the grill. Done.
- **Cast Iron Skillet.** Remove food scraps using a spatula. Next, reheat the cast iron skillet and scrub the surface with coarse salt and oil. That's it!

ONE AND DONE

- **Plug and Play.** Cook the entire meal, snack, or dessert all at once inside a single device like a pressure cooker, air fryer, or slow cooker, leaving only one item to be cleaned afterward.
- **First Apartment Style.** I moved into my first place without much cookware. As a result, I had to get creative when fixing something to eat. My breakfast might be cooked and served in the same cup I used earlier to drink my morning coffee. This unique method is perfect for making personalized portions like a mug cake dessert!

CLEAN AS YOU GO

My family is always being pulled many different directions. As soon as dinner is over, the whole family (including the dog) walks our son to swim practice. There isn't a lot of extra time to waste on cleanup—I'm sure you can relate. Your time is valuable.

Instead of waiting until the meal is finished to determine who will do the dishes, let me suggest an alternative. Tidy up as you go! This isn't as hard (or painful) as you might think. Follow these easy suggestions and stop arguing over whose turn it is. The kitchen will be clean in seconds flat.

- **Wet and Wild.** Keep dirty dishes wet. A little soap and water added NOW prevent the dreaded crustiness from occurring LATER!
- **Multitask.** In between cooking steps, make productive use of your time. Rinse/dry/put away dishes that were only lightly used (like a measuring cup used to measure dry ingredients or a cutting board used briefly to chop vegetables). Not every dish needs to be run through the dishwasher. Sometimes, a quick rinse and dry is all it needs. If an item requires a deeper clean, like after touching raw meat, quickly give it a rinse and immediately load it into the dishwasher.
- **Family Rule.** As a household, agree that eating a meal doesn't begin until an agreed-upon standard has been met. For example, "No one eats dinner until all pots and pans that were used are washed and dried" or "All dishes (currently in the sink) must be loaded into the dishwasher before anyone sits down at the table." It's amazing how motivated and helpful your family can become when they are hungry!

ASK FOR HELP...(OR NOT)?

My kitchen is tiny. Since there isn't a lot of room, I tend to ferociously protect my space. Inviting others into my domain under the guise of "helping" would backfire and ultimately slow me down. With such limited real estate, there is literally no room available for an extra pair of hands. A crowded kitchen might cause an accident (or a fight, let's be honest). Besides, I've already got the dog underfoot as my dance partner. Even though she sometimes causes me to trip, her 100 percent success rate of cleaning up spills and dropped food makes the interference tolerable.

It's not that I don't want assistance; I really do. But I've discovered more effective ways to get the help I need for cleaning up the kitchen:

- **"I Called It!"** Household members can elect to manage certain cleanup responsibilities permanently. I have found that there are jobs that some people just *like*, and I recommend you capitalize on enthusiasm. As many of you know from reading *The DIRTY, LAZY, KETO® Dirt Cheap Cookbook*, my husband (God bless him!) is the thriftiest person I know. He promptly removes and sorts disposed kitchen packaging, turning so-called "trash" *into cold hard cash*. His commitment to recycling is not only helpful; it's downright AMAZING!

- **Alternate.** Assign specific days to family members for tasks to get done. For example, on odd dates, males are in charge of cleanup, while on even dates, females take over. Be creative to meet your family's needs and lifestyle. A division of labor doesn't have to be fifty-fifty for this strategy to work. You may only cook on weekends, and your partner weekdays, or vice versa. In some relationships, one person cooks, but the other shops and cleans. Do what works for your schedule and individual family dynamic. There is no right or wrong way to divide up kitchen duties as long as everyone is left feeling happy.

- **Routines.** In my experience, tasks that occur at the same time every day are more likely to be completed. Taking out the trash every night after dinner, even if it's not really needed, helps keep up the routine long term. Don't believe me? Try asking a teenager to take out the trash "when it's needed," and you'll watch him transform into a human trash compactor to avoid doing the job. *As needed* often gets lost in translation. In fact, my son believes that phrase means, "I'll take out the trash when Mom threatens to take away my Xbox." To avoid frustration, rely on consistent routines instead. Examples of effective routines include: Never go to sleep with dishes still in the sink, wipe table and counters after every dinner, and so on.

- **Throw It Away.** I realize this last suggestion is extremely controversial. Using disposable paper and cooking products is definitely NOT good for the environment. *You're right about that!* My family diligently recycles everything (as mentioned previously), so in my household, at least, we try to balance using disposable products with painstaking, thorough sorting and recycling of what's in our trash. I don't think trying to be perfect should stop you from taking shortcuts to start cooking. If your decision to eat healthier depends on using paper plates and napkins, then I say, *do it.*

STEPHANIE'S TOP TEN HACKS

Cleanup doesn't have to be a drag. With a little teamwork and planning, you can become more efficient and *even speedy* during kitchen cleanup. My goal is to help you cook healthy meals, true, but I also want to help you simplify mealtime (while having fun). This strategy ensures you'll be likely to repeat the process *all over again*! Feel free to borrow one of my top ten workflow hacks to help keep things speeding along. Share your tips with me too! Post on social media using: @dirtylazyketo #dlkcookbook

1   **Trash Bowl.** Instead of making what seems like hundreds of trips to the kitchen trash can during meal prep, toss dribs and drabs as they arise into a designated trash bowl placed on the countertop (the trash bowl is just a pot or bowl you already dirtied while cooking). Empty the contents of your trash bowl to the main kitchen trash only once, at the very end of cooking your meal.

2   **Extra Trash Bags.** Instead of searching for replacement trash bags, keep extra bags at the bottom of the can. Additionally, toss a few fresh-smelling dryer sheets at the bottom of the trash can to combat foul odors.

3   **Mini Trash Trips.** Where I live, disposable plastic grocery bags from the grocery store are a thing of the past. I covet these disposable bags and store them under my kitchen sink stuffed inside an empty plastic milk jug. These mini grocery bags are perfect for trash that can't wait—that stinky or leaky trash that needs to go to the outside garbage receptacle pronto.

4   **Play Music.** Cleaning is much more fun while your favorite songs are playing!

5   **Silverware Mash-Up.** Instead of manually sorting clean silverware into categories (knife, spoon, fork), store mixed utensils together in a giant heap. *Who really cares?*

6   **Foil.** I buy three sizes of aluminum foil: a standard-sized roll for everyday use regular-sized precut sheets to line small trays, and a heavy-duty, extra-large-sized foil roll for lining baking sheets or (sometimes) the grill. Mama loves a quick, disposable cleanup!

7   **Wipes.** In addition to buying spray disinfectant cleaner and paper towels, I keep dispensers of premoistened disinfectant wipes on hand. I find they are easier (and safer) for my kids to use when wiping down counters or mopping up spills. (In case you're wondering why I buy the more expensive premoistened wipes, I've learned the hard way that little boys and spray bottles don't go together!)

8   **Silicone Bakeware.** Upgrade your Teflon cupcake tins (and other baking dishes) to modern silicone bakeware. Say goodbye to paper cupcake liners; your muffins will pop out fast and easy with a flexible twist of the pan, just like when emptying an ice cube tray.

9   **White Towels.** I replaced my mismatched decorative kitchen towels with more practical white flour-sack towels. They are super absorbent, inexpensive to buy in bulk, and easy to bleach clean in the laundry.

10   **Reusable Cups and Straws.** I thank my teenage daughter for introducing me to washable reusable straws and insulated thermal cups. Rather than pull out a fresh glass each time they want to pour a drink (leaving behind a sink full of barely used cups), my children each have their own Hydro Flask for refilling. They each take great pride in caring for their custom bottle, even going so far as to decorate it with stickers. Reusable cups are great for cleanup, and helpful to the environment.

THE DIRTY, LAZY, KETO RECIPES

Short on Time, Long on Flavor

CHAPTER 5

BREAKFAST

In the morning, I do a lot of *skedaddling*. I'm constantly rushing from one end of the house to the other. The clock is ticking and I'm desperately trying to maximize every second. Did the dog go out yet? *Yes.* Is my lunch packed? *Check.* Is there anything left in the kids' backpacks I need to look at? *Ooops!* I'll have to text the kids—they just left for school. Okay, what about dinner? I glance up at the clock…*I should've left by now!*

If your mornings are as stressful as mine, I'm sure you could benefit from some uberfast tips on how to make a DIRTY, LAZY, KETO breakfast quickly and get out the door fast. **A healthy meal doesn't have to be complicated.** Sometimes food can be made the night before—a quick reheat in the microwave and you're ready to go! Other times, pulling out something from the freezer works just as well. I make yummy treats like chaffles on the weekend (when I have more time) and freeze the extra portions. I can quickly reheat a fabulous breakfast as I'm about to walk out the door.

Redefining what breakfast looks like or how it's made is equally helpful when you're pressed for time. My husband (and coauthor) introduced me to the concept of microwaving scrambled eggs when we first got married. At first I was offended by his bachelor ways! Who scrambles an egg in the microwave? *That's ridiculous.* Two kids and a career later, though? I've embraced the technique. **Speed is sometimes more important than perfection.**

During a recent *DIRTY, LAZY, Girl* podcast recording, my cohost, Dr. Tamara Sniezek, blew my mind when talking about eating a salad for breakfast. A *salad*. Really! Once I stopped laughing, I realized maybe she was onto something here. Who says we have to eat cereal, oatmeal, or toast for breakfast? That advice didn't work out well for me! I've decided to be more open-minded about what I eat in the morning.

> When I'm pinched for time, or eating breakfast on the go, eating healthy food is all that matters.

HOT-FOOTED HOMESTYLE "POTATOES"

Sometimes you may feel like your family isn't being supportive. Changing the habits of other people can be an uphill battle. It's possible, however, that your family isn't trying to be malicious—they just may not understand what DIRTY, LAZY, KETO is all about. For example, my in-laws regularly make homestyle potatoes for breakfast when we come to visit. Potatoes are a vegetable, right? Not so fast! They were curious to try this lower-carb alternative using the potato's distant low-carb cousin—*the radish*!

¼ cup unsalted butter

2 cups chopped (¼"–½" chunks) radishes

½ cup chopped green onions

½ cup thinly sliced green bell pepper

2 tablespoons water

1 teaspoon Creole seasoning

1 In a medium skillet over medium heat, melt butter.

2 Stir in all remaining ingredients and cook 20 minutes covered, stirring regularly until radishes are starting to brown and all liquid has been absorbed.

3 Serve warm on a plate.

NET CARBS	
2G	

SERVES 4	
PER SERVING:	
CALORIES	117
FAT	11G
PROTEIN	1G
SODIUM	376MG
FIBER	1G
CARBOHYDRATES	3G
NET CARBS	2G
SUGAR	2G

TIME	
PREP TIME:	10 MINUTES
COOK TIME:	20 MINUTES
TOTAL TIME:	30 MINUTES

TIPS & OPTIONS

Radishes are what I call one of the Seven Wonders of DIRTY, LAZY, KETO. Darn if they don't taste just like fried potatoes.

For added fiber and fullness, keep the skin on these gems during preparation.

Reboot Hot-Footed Homestyle "Potatoes" in No-Bake "Potato" Soup (see Chapter 6).

EARLY EGGS WITH BENEFITS

NET CARBS

2G

SERVES 4

PER SERVING:
CALORIES	457
FAT	40G
PROTEIN	17G
SODIUM	638MG
FIBER	1G
CARBOHYDRATES	3G
NET CARBS	2G
SUGAR	1G

TIME

PREP TIME:	10 MINUTES
COOK TIME:	15 MINUTES
TOTAL TIME:	25 MINUTES

TIPS & OPTIONS

If a perfectly shaped poached egg is NOT important to you, take a shortcut and poach multiple eggs simultaneously. Cut away and dispose of any egg white strands coming off the poached eggs.

Reboot leftover Hollandaise Sauce by enjoying ASAP Asparagus with "Holiday" Sauce (see Chapter 9).

You have my permission to skip going to the gym today. All that whisking counts as a workout.

When poaching eggs, fresh are best. Make friends with neighbors that have chickens. *That's what I did!*

Enjoying a rich sauce like Hollandaise on my Early Eggs with Benefits feels so rich and decadent! Contrary to what many of us were taught, eating fat will help, not hurt, your weight loss efforts.

Poached Eggs

1 tablespoon white vinegar

4 large eggs

Hollandaise Sauce

2 large egg yolks

½ cup unsalted butter, melted

1 tablespoon 100% lemon juice

¼ teaspoon salt

⅛ teaspoon ground black pepper

Toppings

4 slices Canadian bacon

4 slices Boogie Bread (see recipe in this chapter)

1 teaspoon chopped fresh parsley

1. Make the Poached Eggs: In a large saucepan over medium heat, bring 3"–4" of water to a boil. Stir in vinegar.

2. Over a small bowl, carefully crack 1 egg into a small strainer, draining and discarding any loose egg white. Transfer intact egg yolk with membrane from strainer to a small bowl. Repeat process, creating four small bowls of strained eggs.

3. Using a slotted spoon, gently create a slow swirling vortex in the boiling water in the saucepan. Gently pour 1 egg at a time into the center of the vortex and allow swirling water to cook egg 3½ minutes. Remove poached egg using slotted spoon and set aside. Repeat for remaining eggs.

4. Make the Hollandaise: In the bottom of a double boiler over medium-high heat, add 1" water. Heat until water begins to boil.

5. In the top pan of the double boiler, whisk together egg yolks.

6. Slowly, pour melted butter into sauce, whisking rapidly until desired thickness is achieved. Add lemon juice, salt, and pepper and stir.

7. Remove from heat and set aside.

8. On a large microwave-safe plate, spread out Canadian bacon and microwave on high 1 minute. Place 1 slice bacon on top of 1 slice Boogie Bread. Top bacon slice with 1 poached egg. Repeat with remaining bacon, eggs, and bread.

9. Dollop generous portions of Hollandaise Sauce onto each stack. Sprinkle with parsley. Serve immediately.

ALARM CLOCK CEREAL

NET CARBS

2G

SERVES 1

PER SERVING:

CALORIES	140
FAT	11G
PROTEIN	3G
SODIUM	1MG
FIBER	6G
CARBOHYDRATES	8G
NET CARBS	2G
SUGAR	1G

TIME

PREP TIME:	6 MINUTES
COOK TIME:	2 MINUTES
TOTAL TIME:	8 MINUTES

TIPS & OPTIONS

Take Alarm Clock Cereal on the road to enjoy while traveling. Simply prep the dry ingredients at home, pouring a single serving inside a snack-sized Ziploc bag. Use the in-room coffee maker to heat up the needed water. Clever, right?

Reboot unused portions of Alarm Clock Cereal as Accelerated Acai Bowl toppings (see recipe in this chapter).

Feeling fancy? Top your cereal with sugar-free chocolate chips. Lily's, ChocZero, and Hershey's all make varieties of sugar-free chocolate chips you can try.

Even on the weekends, I'm an early riser. I'm excited to jump out of bed and *start the day*. My family, on the other hand, doesn't always share my enthusiasm. They would prefer I don't bang pots and pans to make breakfast while they are still sleeping. Slackers! When I'm trying to be considerate, my go-to "quiet" meals are either a cup of yogurt (in the summer) or a warm bowl of Alarm Clock Cereal (in the winter). *Shhhh!*

½ cup water

1 tablespoon chia seeds

1 tablespoon unsweetened shredded coconut

1 tablespoon crushed pecans

3 (1-gram) packets 0g net carbs sweetener

⅛ teaspoon ground cinnamon

1   In a microwave-safe cup, add water and microwave on high 2 minutes until boiling.

2   Combine all dry ingredients in a large coffee cup.

3   Carefully add boiling water to cereal mixture and stir. Let cool 4–5 minutes, stirring occasionally until cool enough to eat. Enjoy!

PROMPT PROTEIN PANCAKES

The number of available protein powders on the market is startling. At the grocery store, I've been known to stand in a complete stupor trying to figure out which is which. What a time waster! It's become so ridiculous that I now force myself to only order protein powder online (where I can quickly zero in on the product I want). Don't get me wrong; protein powder is worth the added effort and expense. I find the ingredient invaluable for making morning smoothies and recipes like my favorite Prompt Protein Pancakes. These pancakes give me more energy than Pop-Tarts ever did!

4 large eggs, beaten

¼ cup full-fat cream cheese, softened

1 teaspoon baking powder

3 (19-gram) scoops low-carb vanilla protein powder

¾ cup unsweetened almond milk

⅛ teaspoon salt

1 In a food processor, pulse all ingredients 30–60 seconds until completely blended.

2 Heat a large nonstick skillet over medium heat.

3 Pour pancakes of desired size in skillet, using half the batter, and flip after 3–5 minutes, when bubbles are showing.

4 Remove after 2–3 minutes when starting to brown. Repeat with remaining batter.

5 Serve warm.

NET CARBS

1G

SERVES 4

PER SERVING:

CALORIES	172
FAT	10G
PROTEIN	16G
SODIUM	403MG
FIBER	1G
CARBOHYDRATES	2G
NET CARBS	1G
SUGAR	1G

TIME

PREP TIME:	10 MINUTES
COOK TIME:	16 MINUTES
TOTAL TIME:	26 MINUTES

TIPS & OPTIONS

I recommend topping with butter while still warm.

Feeling frisky? A dollop of rebooted Swoop Cream (see Chapter 11) and a few strawberries will start the day just right! Other creative toppings include sugar-free chocolate chips, blueberries, or (*gasp!*) sugar-free chocolate syrup.

Have you found a sugar-free pancake syrup yet? My all-time favorite is Mrs. Butterworth's. I find it to be the thickest of the available low-carb options on the market.

DELIVERY DONUTS

When I was a kid, my sibling and I clamored to be first to open the door when Gram came to visit. Like any good grandparent, she brought more than just hugs and kisses. Perhaps most important (sorry, Gram!), she held a large container full of homemade red velvet donuts. Everyone tried to steal those Delivery Donuts! My keto-friendly donut recipe has just as much pizazz, but without so many carbs.

½ cup 0g net carbs sweetener

½ cup superfine blanched almond flour

¼ cup coconut flour

2 tablespoons unsweetened 100% cocoa powder

1 teaspoon baking powder

1 teaspoon xanthan gum

⅛ teaspoon ground cayenne pepper

⅛ teaspoon salt

½ cup heavy whipping cream

1 tablespoon full-fat sour cream

1 teaspoon pure vanilla extract

1 large egg, beaten

3 tablespoons coconut oil, melted

2 tablespoons sugar-free chocolate chips

⅓ cup Frantic Vanilla Frosting (see Chapter 11)

2–4 drops red food coloring

1 Preheat oven to 350°F. Grease six donut molds thoroughly with nonstick cooking spray.

2 In a large bowl, combine sweetener, almond flour, coconut flour, cocoa powder, baking powder, xanthan gum, cayenne, and salt and mix well.

3 In a medium bowl, whisk together all remaining ingredients except chocolate chips, frosting, and food coloring.

4 Whisk wet ingredients into dry ingredients. Fold in chocolate chips until thoroughly blended.

5 Transfer batter to a large Ziploc bag and snip 1" from corner.

6 Evenly pipe mixture into prepared donut molds, making six donuts. Bake 23–24 minutes until cooked throughout and starting to brown.

7 In a small bowl, combine frosting and food coloring until well blended and desired color is achieved.

8 While donuts are still warm, spread each with equal amounts of frosting. Frosting will melt like a glaze as donuts cool.

NET CARBS

5G

SERVES 6

PER SERVING:

CALORIES	272
FAT	24G
PROTEIN	6G
SODIUM	177MG
FIBER	5G
CARBOHYDRATES	13G
NET CARBS	5G
SUGAR	2G
SUGAR ALCOHOL	3G

TIME

PREP TIME:	6 MINUTES
COOK TIME:	24 MINUTES
TOTAL TIME:	30 MINUTES

TIPS & OPTIONS

Top with chopped nuts, shredded unsweetened coconut, or sugar-free chocolate chips before frosting dries to "lock 'em in good."

Gallon-sized or freezer-grade Ziploc bags work best for makeshift pastry bags. Anything smaller is likely to split at the seams when pressure is used to squeeze out the batter.

BOOGIE BREAD

NET CARBS

1G

SERVES 2

PER SERVING:

CALORIES	150
FAT	14G
PROTEIN	5G
SODIUM	131MG
FIBER	1G
CARBOHYDRATES	2G
NET CARBS	1G
SUGAR	0G

TIME

PREP TIME:	5 MINUTES
COOK TIME:	10 MINUTES
TOTAL TIME:	15 MINUTES

TIPS & OPTIONS

Since Boogie Bread is savory, not sweet, use as "toast" to accompany your morning eggs.

Top Boogie Bread with butter, peanut butter, or sugar-free jam. One of my favorites is Smucker's Sugar Free Seedless Blackberry Jam, which has 3 grams net carbs per 1-tablespoon serving.

Prefer a breakfast sandwich to go? Use Boogie Bread as the "bread" with eggs, sausage, and cheese stuffed inside.

Reboot Boogie Bread in Rush In Reuben (see Chapter 10) or Early Eggs with Benefits (see recipe in this chapter).

Intermittent fasting (also referred to as I.F.) is all the rage these days. It can be interpreted different ways, but in my mind, I.F. is a fancy way of saying, "No eating after dinner, Stephanie." Call it whatever you want, but this strategy is effective. No good decisions about food are made late at night—*at least in my kitchen*! Plus, as an added benefit, I wake up the next morning motivated (and hungry!) to make a quick, healthy breakfast like Boogie Bread.

1 large egg, beaten

1 tablespoon water

2 tablespoons superfine blanched almond flour

1½ tablespoons full-fat mayonnaise

⅛ teaspoon baking powder

1 Lightly grease a waffle maker with nonstick cooking spray and preheat.

2 In a medium bowl, whisk all ingredients together.

3 Pour half the batter in center of waffle maker and close. Cook 3–5 minutes until solid and browning. Remove and repeat for second Boogie Bread.

4 Serve warm.

DOUBLE-QUICK DOUBLE-CHOCOLATE CHAFFLES

As a kid, I remember thinking frozen waffles were such a waste of time. All I really wanted was the syrup! I can't imagine going back to those kinds of habits. A plate full of carbs, carbs, and topped with more carbs? No thanks. I want to be awake in an hour, not feeling my blood sugar go haywire. This adult version of DIRTY, LAZY, KETO waffles, Double-Quick Double-Chocolate Chaffles, fulfills my desire for morning sweets but without leaving me in a blood-sugar crash.

2 tablespoons superfine blanched almond flour

2 tablespoons full-fat cream cheese, softened

1 tablespoon unsweetened 100% cocoa powder

1 tablespoon sugar-free chocolate chips

1 large egg, beaten

2 (1-gram) packets 0g net carbs sweetener

1 teaspoon pure vanilla extract

1. Lightly grease a waffle maker with nonstick cooking spray and preheat.

2. In a medium bowl, whisk all ingredients together.

3. Pour half of batter in center of waffle maker and close. Cook 3–5 minutes until solid and browning. Remove and repeat for second chaffle.

4. Serve warm.

NET CARBS
2G

SERVES 2

PER SERVING:

CALORIES	167
FAT	13G
PROTEIN	7G
SODIUM	88MG
FIBER	4G
CARBOHYDRATES	8G
NET CARBS	2G
SUGAR	1G
SUGAR ALCOHOL	2G

TIME

PREP TIME:	10 MINUTES
COOK TIME:	10 MINUTES
TOTAL TIME:	20 MINUTES

TIPS & OPTIONS

In case the Double-Quick Double-Chocolate Chaffles don't have enough chocolate for ya (*is there ever such a thing as too much chocolate?*), try topping with a dollop of Swoop Cream (see Chapter 11) and Hershey's Sugar-Free Syrup (1 gram net carbs per 1-tablespoon serving).

SWIFT CINNAMON ROLLS

NET CARBS

2G

SERVES 6

PER SERVING:

CALORIES	248
FAT	20G
PROTEIN	8G
SODIUM	326MG
FIBER	2G
CARBOHYDRATES	9G
NET CARBS	2G
SUGAR	1G
SUGAR ALCOHOL	5G

TIME

PREP TIME:	10 MINUTES
COOK TIME:	20 MINUTES
TOTAL TIME:	30 MINUTES

TIPS & OPTIONS ≫

If you've ever been to a Cinnabon Bakery, you'll know the employees ask if you want frosting on top of your roll. *Who in their right mind says no?* I won't be able to sleep tonight unless I share how to make Frantic Vanilla Frosting (see Chapter 11) for this recipe.

If your rolls don't cooperate during cutting, try freezing the dough for a few minutes to firm up.

Research from a perfume company proved what I already knew to be true: The scents of vanilla and cinnamon are preferred over all other scents. My personal market research was unofficially conducted at the mall the other day when I found myself blindly drawn to the wafting smells from the Cinnabon walk-up. I'm like a moth to a flame when it comes to *deliciousness* of this caliber. Fix up a batch of Swift Cinnamon Rolls and watch your family swarm around.

Dough

3 tablespoons full-fat cream cheese

1 cup shredded whole milk mozzarella cheese

⅔ cup superfine blanched almond flour

3 tablespoons 0g net carbs sweetener

1 large egg, beaten

1 teaspoon pure vanilla extract

½ tablespoon baking powder

⅛ teaspoon salt

Buttery Sweetener

¼ cup unsalted butter, melted

2 tablespoons 0g net carbs sweetener

1 teaspoon ground cinnamon

1. Preheat oven to 375°F. Grease a baking sheet.

2. In a medium microwave-safe bowl, add cream cheese and mozzarella and microwave on high 30 seconds. Stir until blended.

3. Add remaining Dough ingredients and stir to combine until a dough forms. Roll the dough flat on a large piece of plastic wrap. Form a rectangle approximately 10" × 6" and no more than ¼" thick. Dough will be sticky.

4. In a small bowl, combine Buttery Sweetener ingredients. Whisk to mix thoroughly.

5. Brush half the Buttery Sweetener on Dough and roll tightly starting at one of the short sides, creating a loaf 6" long.

6. Using a serrated knife or thin string (like dental floss), cut loaf into six rolls, 1" wide. Carefully transfer rolls to baking sheet and top with remaining Buttery Sweetener.

7. Bake 15–18 minutes until golden.

8. Let cool slightly and serve warm.

MINUTE MUG OMELET

Mornings can be stressful. Trying to get everyone ready and out the door on time can lead to hasty decision-making when it comes to healthy eating (making that break room pastry look ever so tempting!). You won't go down that path, though, if you embrace a few shortcuts in the morning. Put your hair in a ponytail *or man-bun* and start crackin' some shells. Cooked in the microwave, this Minute Mug Omelet will be ready in no time.

2 large eggs
2 tablespoons unsweetened almond milk
2 tablespoons shredded Cheddar cheese
2 tablespoons diced green bell pepper
1 tablespoon chopped ham
⅛ teaspoon salt
⅛ teaspoon ground black pepper

1. Grease a large microwave-safe coffee mug.
2. Add eggs to prepared mug and beat, using a fork.
3. Beat in remaining ingredients until completely mixed.
4. Cover and microwave omelet on high 45 seconds.
5. Stir, cover, and microwave again 30 seconds.
6. Enjoy warm right out of the mug.

FLEETING FRENCH TOAST

Hands down, French toast brings back the best memories from childhood. Whenever it was my turn to choose what we were having for dinner (which was pretty rare!), I chose French toast. Topped with a snowy drift of confectioners' sugar, it was pastry in disguise. One of the best parts of DIRTY, LAZY, KETO is that I don't have to give up any of these indulgences. The only difference is that I've learned how to remake my breakfast favorites in a healthier way.

NET CARBS
3G

SERVES 2

PER SERVING:

CALORIES	256
FAT	21G
PROTEIN	9G
SODIUM	230MG
FIBER	3G
CARBOHYDRATES	7G
NET CARBS	3G
SUGAR	2G
SUGAR ALCOHOL	1G

TIME

PREP TIME:	10 MINUTES
COOK TIME:	7 MINUTES, 30 SECONDS
TOTAL TIME:	17 MINUTES, 30 SECONDS

TIPS & OPTIONS

Some great suggestions for toppings are pecans, sliced strawberries, or sugar-free pancake syrup.

When you fool the eye, you fool the palate. Sprinkle confectioners'-style 0g net carbs sweetener on top of your serving of Fleeting French Toast for the most dramatic and authentic presentation.

Bread

1½ tablespoons unsalted butter, melted

2 tablespoons coconut flour

1 tablespoon full-fat cream cheese, softened

1 large egg, beaten

½ teaspoon baking powder

French Toast Coating

1 large egg, beaten

2 tablespoons heavy whipping cream

¼ teaspoon ground cinnamon

1 teaspoon 0g net carbs sweetener

¼ teaspoon pure vanilla extract

1 In a medium microwave-safe dish, add all Bread ingredients and stir to combine.

2 Microwave on high 1½ minutes, then remove from microwave and allow to cool. Cut in half.

3 In a separate medium bowl, whisk together all French Toast Coating ingredients until sweetener is dissolved. Pour mixture onto a plate.

4 Place both pieces of bread on the plate to soak. Flip after 30 seconds to soak other side.

5 Heat a medium nonstick skillet over medium heat. Add both pieces of bread and fry 2–3 minutes on each side until brown and crispy.

6 Serve warm.

ACCELERATED ACAI BOWL

On family vacations, we often stop at a food court for lunch. Everyone can get what they want, right? One meal in particular was a showstopper. My daughter waited in the longest line (with all the cool kids) and brought back a lunch that looked more like a dessert than a meal. The color scheme alone was impressive! I spent the rest of our trip trying to pronounce acai (ah-sah-EE) and scheming how to make a low-carb version back at home.

1½ cups plain full-fat Greek yogurt

½ teaspoon acai powder

2 teaspoons 0g net carbs sweetener

1 tablespoon chia seeds

¼ cup sliced strawberries

¼ cup raspberries

2 tablespoons crushed pecans

1 tablespoon unsweetened shredded coconut, toasted

½ tablespoon finely chopped dark chocolate, 92% cacao

1   In a small bowl, whisk together yogurt, acai powder, sweetener, and chia seeds.

2   Divide mixture evenly between two medium bowls.

3   Top bowls with remaining ingredients in an artful manner.

4   Cover and let chill in the refrigerator at least 20 minutes to allow chia seeds to soften.

5   Serve chilled.

NET CARBS

9G

SERVES 2

PER SERVING:

CALORIES	268
FAT	18G
PROTEIN	17G
SODIUM	60MG
FIBER	3G
CARBOHYDRATES	12G
NET CARBS	9G
SUGAR	8G

TIME

PREP TIME:	30 MINUTES
COOK TIME:	0 MINUTES
TOTAL TIME:	30 MINUTES

TIPS & OPTIONS

Acai berries are mainstream, baby! Forget the health food store; find this superfood at supermarkets everywhere.

Carefully design your Accelerated Acai Bowl with the goal of posting a picture of it on social media (you're one of the cool kids now).

In case you're curious, the potent acai berries come from the acai palm, which thrives in the Amazon River delta. Not only does the tree provide berries rich in antioxidants, but the core of the palm is harvested for heart of palm, a delicious (though arguably pricey) noodle alternative.

SHORTCUT CINNAMON TOAST STICKS

A surefire way to get my kids up and moving before school is to make Shortcut Cinnamon Toast Sticks. There is something about the blended aromas of vanilla and cinnamon in the air—the smell is so tantalizing it can wake up the dead (or very tired teenagers... *so*, basically the same thing). Serve these warm with sugar-free pancake syrup as a dip.

2 large eggs, beaten

1 cup shredded whole milk mozzarella cheese

2 tablespoons 0g net carbs sweetener

1½ teaspoons ground cinnamon

1 Grease a waffle maker with nonstick cooking spray and preheat.

2 In a medium mixing bowl, whisk eggs and mozzarella.

3 If using a single waffle maker, pour one-third of egg mixture into waffle maker and cook 3 minutes until browned and solid throughout. Transfer to a plate and slice into even strips no more than ¾" wide. Repeat with remaining batter.

4 While first piece of toast is cooking, combine sweetener and cinnamon on a shallow plate.

5 Roll still-warm toast strips in cinnamon mixture. Coat both sides and shake off any excess.

6 Serve immediately.

CHAPTER 6

SOUPS AND SALADS

It may be due to my middle-aged hormone problems—I'm not sure—but the temperature outside often dictates the method I prefer to cook with. When I'm freezing, I crave warm soups, stews, and chilis; slow cookers and stockpots become my best friends. On the other hand, hot weather makes me run from the kitchen. I refuse to even turn on my oven during the summer months! Because of my erratic inner thermostat, I often waver between making DIRTY, LAZY, KETO soups or salads for dinner.

You can revise any of your family's favorite soup recipes to become DIRTY, LAZY, KETO by following a few simple steps. Substitute offending high-starch ingredients like rice, potatoes, or beans with a low-carb alternative. Riced cauliflower (added at the last minute) fools the mouth and brain into thinking that you are eating rice. Boiled radishes or softened cauliflower florets resemble potato chunks when floating in sauce. Lastly, instead of making soup with high-carb black beans, try low-carb black soybeans instead. *Be creative!* Next, to increase the amount of fats in your soup, add intense flavor by stirring in additional cream cheese, olive oil, or cream to the soup stock. *That's it!* Simple and fast.

Quickly assembling a DIRTY, LAZY, KETO salad is all about having the right ingredients on hand. Once you stock these items in your fridge, it takes only a few minutes to toss desired flavors together and artfully present them on a plate. Salad ingredients I keep on hand include prewashed bagged salad greens, assorted cheeses, and leftover protein (hard-boiled eggs, grilled chicken, turkey lunch meat, etc.). Berries, nuts, and various chopped veggies make tasty additions to an otherwise "blah" salad. Don't be afraid to cut corners by using store-bought salad dressings either. When I'm pressed for time, I gladly pour purchased low-carb salad dressings (like ranch or blue cheese) over my salad and get started with the fun part—*eating*!

GASSED-UP CHILI

"This tastes like nothing," my son said to me when describing cauliflower. And you know what? He is right. Cauliflower magically takes on the flavors of whatever foods surround it, making it the most versatile vegetable in the DIRTY, LAZY, KETO universe. When added to this Gassed-Up Chili dish, the florets provide the perfect amount of bulk and texture without sacrificing taste.

- **1 medium head cauliflower, cut into bite-sized florets**
- **2 tablespoons unsalted butter**
- **1 medium yellow onion, peeled and chopped**
- **1 large green bell pepper, seeded and chopped**
- **1 recipe Ready, Set, Go Ground Beef (see Chapter 10)**
- **2 (8-ounce) cans no-sugar-added tomato sauce**
- **½ tablespoon minced garlic**
- **2 teaspoons chili powder**
- **1½ teaspoons ground cumin**
- **¼ teaspoon paprika**
- **¼ teaspoon salt**
- **¼ teaspoon ground black pepper**

1. In a medium microwave-safe bowl, add cauliflower and microwave on high 4–5 minutes until tender.
2. In a large soup pot over medium heat, melt butter. Stir in onion and bell pepper and cook 5 minutes until softened.
3. Stir in cauliflower and remaining ingredients and bring to a boil. Reduce heat to low and simmer covered 10 minutes.
4. Remove from heat and let cool uncovered. Serve warm.

NET CARBS

8G

SERVES 6

PER SERVING:

CALORIES	211
FAT	9G
PROTEIN	20G
SODIUM	664MG
FIBER	6G
CARBOHYDRATES	14G
NET CARBS	8G
SUGAR	6G

TIME

PREP TIME:	10 MINUTES
COOK TIME:	20 MINUTES
TOTAL TIME:	30 MINUTES

TIPS & OPTIONS

Make a chili dog! Reboot Gassed-Up Chili over hot dogs from the grill to make Convenient Chili-Cheese Dogs from Chapter 7.

Serve chili in a bag? Yes, you can! Crush a bag of Quest Nacho Cheese Tortilla Style Protein Chips. Carefully cut open the bag with scissors along the top. Pour chili inside the bag and serve.

NO FUSS PHO

You may wonder why I include so many Asian dishes in the DIRTY, LAZY, KETO cookbooks. On the whole, I find Eastern cuisine embraces vegetables much more than the Western diet, where French fries are practically their own food group. Since I believe that vegetables are the magic elixir needed for weight loss, I look for as many ways as possible to incorporate low-carb veggies into my meals. Dishes like No Fuss Pho are a quick and obvious vehicle to make this possible.

½ cup chopped green onions, divided

1 tablespoon minced fresh ginger

6 cups beef broth

½ tablespoon minced garlic

1 tablespoon soy sauce

2 (8-ounce) packages shirataki noodles

1 pound flank steak, thinly sliced

¼ cup bean sprouts

1 medium jalapeño pepper, seeded, deveined, and sliced in rings

½ tablespoon chopped fresh cilantro

½ tablespoon chopped fresh basil

1   In a medium nonstick skillet over medium heat, add ¼ cup onion and ginger. Cook 5 minutes while stirring until brown. Transfer to a large soup pot.

2   Place soup pot over medium heat. Add broth, garlic, and soy sauce. Bring to a boil, then reduce heat to low and simmer 10 minutes.

3   Divide remaining ingredients evenly among four bowls.

4   Carefully ladle broth mixture into bowls. The near-boiling broth will cook meat as well as other vegetables.

5   Enjoy when cool enough to taste.

NET CARBS	
1G	
SERVES 4	
PER SERVING:	
CALORIES	221
FAT	8G
PROTEIN	29G
SODIUM	1,632MG
FIBER	4G
CARBOHYDRATES	5G
NET CARBS	1G
SUGAR	1G

TIME	
PREP TIME:	15 MINUTES
COOK TIME:	15 MINUTES
TOTAL TIME:	30 MINUTES

TIPS & OPTIONS

Pho isn't just fun to eat; it's an interesting word to say. *Pho* is pronounced *fuh*.

I don't usually eat shirataki noodles, but for this pho dish, I make an exception. Fans of these fishy noodles asked me to create a pho recipe, and I aim to please. If you're like me and the scent of these throw you for a loop, try substituting zucchini noodles (zoodles) instead.

Pick up your bowl and slurp away—totally acceptable in Vietnamese culture.

YOU SNOOZE, YOU LOSE ALFREDO SOUP

Eating healthy doesn't have to take up a lot of time. Once you have the right ingredients on hand, putting them together becomes easier. Aside from fresh vegetables, there's a handful of ingredients I'm never without: butter, cream cheese, eggs, Parmesan cheese, and heavy whipping cream. I don't eat these in excess, mind you, but I find that most recipes call for one or another of these from this list. As demonstrated by this You Snooze, You Lose Alfredo Soup, cooking with full-fat ingredients creates a rich and satisfying taste. I feel fuller faster and end up eating less food overall as a result.

2 tablespoons unsalted butter

1 medium yellow onion, peeled and chopped

2 teaspoons minced garlic

6 tablespoons full-fat cream cheese

⅔ cup heavy whipping cream

½ cup grated Parmesan cheese

2 cups chopped Grab and Go Chicken Breasts (see Chapter 10)

2½ cups chopped broccoli florets

2 cups chicken broth

2 teaspoons Italian seasoning

¼ teaspoon salt

⅛ teaspoon ground black pepper

1 In a large soup pot over medium heat, melt butter.

2 Stir in onion and garlic and cook 5 minutes until soft.

3 Stir in remaining ingredients and bring to a boil while stirring. Reduce heat and simmer covered 15 minutes, stirring regularly.

4 Serve warm.

NET CARBS

6G

SERVES 6

PER SERVING:
CALORIES	285
FAT	20G
PROTEIN	15G
SODIUM	685MG
FIBER	1G
CARBOHYDRATES	7G
NET CARBS	6G
SUGAR	3G

TIME

PREP TIME:	10 MINUTES
COOK TIME:	20 MINUTES
TOTAL TIME:	30 MINUTES

TIPS & OPTIONS

Once a week at the grocery store, I buy a rotisserie chicken. Having the precooked protein on hand makes cooking dinner a snap! In my community, Costco sells cooked "astronaut chickens" for less than five bucks a bird.

MINESTRONE ZIPPY ZOODLE SOUP

Zoodles fascinate me. How can a zucchini become a noodle? It's amazing! The best part is how quickly you can make a zoodle. (Don't get swept up in the hype about commercial zoodle makers, now!). A simple julienne peeler is all you need to create spiralized noodles in under a minute. They will cook in a flash and take your Minestrone Zippy Zoodle Soup to the next level.

1 tablespoon olive oil

1½ cups chopped celery

2 tablespoons chopped green onion

½ tablespoon minced garlic

4 cups chicken broth

2 tablespoons white vinegar

¼ teaspoon salt

⅛ teaspoon ground black pepper

1 pound boneless, skinless chicken breasts

1½ cups spiralized zucchini

1   Add oil to Instant Pot® and heat using Sauté function at Less setting. Stir in celery, green onions, and garlic and cook 5 minutes while stirring.

2   Stir in broth, vinegar, salt, and pepper until combined. Arrange chicken breasts evenly over mixture.

3   Put on lid and close pressure release. Cook on High Pressure 10 minutes.

4   Carefully quick-release pressure and remove lid to cool.

5   Using two forks, shred cooked chicken in Instant Pot®.

6   Add zucchini and stir to combine. Using Sauté function at Normal setting, cook 5 minutes while stirring.

7   Turn off heat and let cool with lid off. Serve warm.

NET CARBS

2G

SERVES 6

PER SERVING:

CALORIES	132
FAT	4G
PROTEIN	19G
SODIUM	769MG
FIBER	1G
CARBOHYDRATES	3G
NET CARBS	2G
SUGAR	2G

TIME

PREP TIME:	10 MINUTES
COOK TIME:	20 MINUTES
TOTAL TIME:	30 MINUTES

TIPS & OPTIONS

If you can swing it, add fresh herbs like minced fresh parsley, rosemary, and thyme to the broth. It will smell *ahhhhhhmaaaazzzinnnng*!

My family loves when I make a theme-night dinner like Unlimited Soup and Salad. It sounds special and we all fill up on healthy food.

Reboot leftover zoodles to make the EZ Zoodle Noodle "Spaghetti" recipe in Chapter 10.

FAST-TRACK FRENCH ONION SOUP

TIPS & OPTIONS

Instead of white wine, substitute a splash of brandy in your broth à la Julia Child style.

Make the soup vegetarian-"ish" by using vegetable broth instead of beef.

If you don't want to buy a whole package of Gruyère cheese, try buying just the right amount at the fresh deli counter inside your supermarket.

Gruyère is a bit of a "grown-up" cheese (and subsequently can be pricey or hard to find). Feel free to substitute sliced Swiss cheese.

There are a few topics that really get the keto police riled up. Diet soda, carrots, and onions rank right up there. (*Sad but true! Get a life, people.*) The food police love to share unsolicited nutrition advice like, "Onions are NOT keto!" I'm going to fight back here with my Fast-Track French Onion Soup. If enjoyed in moderation, onions add flavor and fun to my cooking. This recipe is my way of saying, "Nanny nanny boo boo" to all the negative ninnies who criticize my beloved onion.

2 tablespoons unsalted butter

1 medium white onion, peeled and thinly sliced

1 bunch green onions (approximately 6), trimmed and chopped

1 tablespoon minced garlic

⅛ teaspoon salt

4 cups beef broth

¼ cup white wine

¼ teaspoon ground thyme

2 bay leaves

½ teaspoon ground black pepper

4 (1-ounce) slices Gruyère cheese

¼ cup grated Parmesan cheese

1   In a medium skillet over medium-low heat, melt butter.

2   Add onions, garlic, and salt. Cook until caramelized, about 10 minutes.

3   While onion mixture is cooking, in a microwave-safe bowl, add broth. Microwave on high 2–3 minutes until boiling.

4   Add broth to skillet, then add all remaining ingredients except cheeses. Reduce heat to low and simmer an additional 10 minutes.

5   Preheat broiler to high.

6   Place four small oven-safe bowls inside a large baking dish (for transporting to broiler).

7   Evenly distribute soup among four bowls. Remove bay leaves. Top each bowl with 1 slice Gruyère, draping over edges of bowl. Top with equal amounts Parmesan.

8   Place tray of soups under broiler 1–2 minutes until cheese browns. Serve warm.

NO PATIENCE POLLO SOUP

NET CARBS

5G

SERVES 4

PER SERVING:

CALORIES	317
FAT	18G
PROTEIN	25G
SODIUM	1,060MG
FIBER	4G
CARBOHYDRATES	9G
NET CARBS	5G
SUGAR	3G

TIME

PREP TIME:	10 MINUTES
COOK TIME:	20 MINUTES
TOTAL TIME:	30 MINUTES

TIPS & OPTIONS

To make the soup heartier, add riced cauliflower.

Sour cream, shredded Cheddar cheese, and olives are suggested low-carb soup toppings.

If you don't have a pressure cooker, make No Patience Pollo Soup on your stovetop using a large covered stockpot. Boil until chicken is thoroughly cooked, about 30 minutes for boneless thighs and 45 minutes for bone-in thighs.

Cooking with a pressure cooker is life-changing. It's removed all of my excuses for not having enough time to make dinner! I mean, really. The fact that you can cook a frozen piece of meat in just minutes is shocking. Who figured this out? *Someone hungry, that's who!* I don't want to spend all day in the kitchen making dinner. I want to throw a handful of ingredients into a pot without much fuss. No Patience Pollo Soup looks fancy and tastes yummy, but most important, it cooks quickly while I check *Facebook*.

1 pound boneless, skinless chicken thighs, sliced

1 (10-ounce) can no-sugar-added diced tomatoes and green chiles

2 cups chicken broth

2 tablespoons unsalted butter

¼ cup chopped green onion

2 teaspoons minced garlic

½ tablespoon onion powder

1 teaspoon chili powder

½ teaspoon ground cumin

½ tablespoon paprika

½ medium jalapeño pepper, seeded, deveined, and diced

½ teaspoon salt

1 medium avocado, peeled, pitted, and sliced

1 tablespoon chopped fresh cilantro

1   In Instant Pot®, combine all ingredients except avocado and cilantro. Stir to mix.

2   Put on lid and close pressure release. Cook on High Pressure 20 minutes. Carefully quick-release pressure and remove lid. Stir to mix well.

3   Serve warm topped with avocado slices and sprinkle of cilantro.

LIGHTNING-SPEED SLAW

I get SUPER excited at social events when my DIRTY, LAZY, KETO dishes rub shoulders with high-carb counterparts on the buffet line. I can almost feel the scrutiny and suspicion from critical family members and friends deciding how to fill their plate (trying to avoid suspicious "diet food"). I see this as a challenge to prove them wrong. Lightning-Speed Slaw is so rich and satisfying, even Grandma will think it's *the real thing*.

1 (16-ounce) bag coleslaw mix

⅓ cup full-fat mayonnaise

1 tablespoon apple cider vinegar

1 teaspoon 100% lemon juice

1 tablespoon 0g net carbs sweetener

¼ teaspoon salt

⅛ teaspoon ground black pepper

1   In a large bowl, add coleslaw mix.

2   In a medium bowl, combine all remaining ingredients. Stir to thoroughly mix.

3   Using a spatula, add dressing to coleslaw mix. Stir to combine.

4   Cover and put in refrigerator until ready to serve. Serve chilled.

NET CARBS	
4G	
SERVES 5	
PER SERVING:	
CALORIES	124
FAT	11G
PROTEIN	1G
SODIUM	225MG
FIBER	2G
CARBOHYDRATES	7G
NET CARBS	4G
SUGAR	3G
SUGAR ALCOHOL	1G

TIME	
PREP TIME:	10 MINUTES
COOK TIME:	0 MINUTES
TOTAL TIME:	10 MINUTES

TIPS & OPTIONS

Adjust the sweetener to your taste.

Adjust the vegetables and spices as you wish. Green onion, red onion, and parsley are all great choices.

Sometimes I top my coleslaw with a tablespoon of sunflower seeds. They add just the right amount of crunch with a punch of salt to the sweet dressing.

NO-BAKE "POTATO" SOUP

DLK is full of surprises. For example, there's no potato in this soup, but the cauliflower florets and vibrant radish skins will fool you into thinking that there is. Radishes are the ideal potato substitute. I'm certain they will become a keto staple in your household too. I use radishes so often in recipes that now I keep extra servings of this prepped veggie on hand for moments like this. (See the Hot-Footed Homestyle "Potatoes" recipe in Chapter 5.) Radishes are truly the secret ingredient of No-Bake "Potato" Soup!

1 (12-ounce) bag frozen cauliflower pieces, broken into bite-sized florets

2 tablespoons unsalted butter

1 cup finely chopped radishes

1 cup sliced zucchini

½ cup chopped green onions, divided

1 tablespoon minced garlic

4 cups chicken broth

½ cup full-fat cream cheese

2 (3.7-gram) chicken-flavored bouillon cubes

⅛ teaspoon ground black pepper

2 cups shredded Cheddar cheese

¼ cup cooked bacon bits

1 In a large microwave-safe dish, add cauliflower. Cover and microwave on high 4–5 minutes until tender.

2 While cauliflower cooks, in a large soup pot over medium heat, melt butter. Add radishes, zucchini, ¼ cup onion, and garlic. Sauté 3–4 minutes until softened.

3 Add cauliflower, broth, cream cheese, bouillon, and pepper to soup pot. Bring covered pot to a boil, then reduce heat to low and simmer 20 minutes while stirring.

4 Using an immersion blender, pulse soup ingredients 1–2 minutes to desired consistency.

5 Add Cheddar to soup and fold in.

6 Pour into six small bowls and top with equal amounts bacon bits and remaining green onion. Serve immediately.

NET CARBS

5G

SERVES 6

PER SERVING:

CALORIES	310
FAT	22G
PROTEIN	15G
SODIUM	1,354MG
FIBER	2G
CARBOHYDRATES	7G
NET CARBS	5G
SUGAR	4G

TIME

PREP TIME:	5 MINUTES
COOK TIME:	25 MINUTES
TOTAL TIME:	30 MINUTES

TIPS & OPTIONS

For a heartier soup, top with your choice of protein. I like to add leftover taco meat, shredded chicken, or basically any leftovers from last night's meal.

Don't have an immersion blender? Though messy (and hot!), here is a work-around. Transfer soup to a standing blender in small batches and pulse until desired consistency is achieved.

Be careful not to over-blend your soup. Bites of cauliflower and radish will fool your brain into thinking you're eating baby red potatoes.

HURRY UP HOUSE SALAD WITH RANCH

NET CARBS

4G

SERVES 8

PER SERVING:	
CALORIES	92
FAT	8G
PROTEIN	1G
SODIUM	83MG
FIBER	1G
CARBOHYDRATES	5G
NET CARBS	4G
SUGAR	3G

TIME

PREP TIME:	15 MINUTES
COOK TIME:	0 MINUTES
TOTAL TIME:	15 MINUTES

TIPS & OPTIONS ≫

Substitute your favorite low-carb salad vegetables and toppings. Go heavy on what's in season and available in your fridge.

Set some dressing aside for later in the week to use as a dip when it's time for pizza! Or chicken! Or…just about anything!

Ranch is like a food group when you come from the Midwest. Don't judge, but we like ranch on just about everything, from pizza to wings to veggies. As such, I take my ranch dressing seriously. There was a time in my life when on my way home from work, I would drive out of the way just to get to the best pizza parlor, simply because it had the most spectacular ranch dressing. I've had to endure hundreds of taste tests (such a rough job) to get this one right.

DLK House Salad

1 (24-ounce) bag salad mix

1 medium red onion, peeled and chopped

1 cup grape tomatoes, halved

DLK House Ranch Dressing Mix

¼ cup dried parsley flakes

2 tablespoons 0g net carbs sweetener

3½ tablespoons dried garlic flakes

1½ tablespoons onion powder

1½ tablespoons lemon pepper

1 tablespoon dried dill

1 teaspoon salt

DLK House Ranch Dressing

¼ cup full-fat mayonnaise

¼ cup full-fat sour cream

1 tablespoon 100% lemon juice

1 tablespoon DLK House Ranch Dressing Mix

2 tablespoons water

2 tablespoons heavy whipping cream

⅛ teaspoon ground black pepper

1. In a large salad bowl, add all DLK House Salad ingredients.

2. In a medium bowl, add all DLK House Ranch Dressing Mix ingredients and stir until mixed. For storage, put in an airtight container (preferably a transparent one, so mix can be seen). Store in the spice rack with the rest of your spices.

3. In a medium bowl, whisk all DLK House Ranch Dressing ingredients together.

4. Using a rubber spatula, pour the DLK House Ranch Dressing on top of the DLK House Salad and toss well to coat. Cover and put in refrigerator until ready to serve.

5. Serve chilled in fancy salad bowls.

INSTAMATIC CUCUMBER SALAD

One of my favorite mantras with DIRTY, LAZY, KETO is to "use fat to make healthy food taste better." Let's face it. Most of us don't wake up in the morning craving a cucumber. *Let's be real!* But when it's chopped up into Instamatic Cucumber Salad with full-fat mayonnaise and sour cream? Now that's a whole different story. Fat makes everything taste better. Use that to your advantage! Pair fats with low-carb veggies and watch your waistline shrink.

2 medium cucumbers, skin on and sliced

½ medium red onion, peeled and chopped

2 tablespoons full-fat sour cream

2 tablespoons full-fat mayonnaise

2 teaspoons 100% lemon juice

1 medium clove garlic, peeled and minced

¼ teaspoon salt

⅛ teaspoon ground black pepper

2 teaspoons finely chopped fresh cilantro

1   In a medium bowl, add cucumbers and onion.

2   In a small bowl, whisk to combine remaining ingredients.

3   Pour dressing on top of vegetables and stir to coat.

4   Cover with wrap and put in refrigerator. Give final stir prior to serving chilled.

NET CARBS

6G

SERVES 4

PER SERVING:

CALORIES	87
FAT	6G
PROTEIN	1G
SODIUM	195MG
FIBER	1G
CARBOHYDRATES	7G
NET CARBS	6G
SUGAR	3G

TIME

PREP TIME:	10 MINUTES
COOK TIME:	0 MINUTES
TOTAL TIME:	10 MINUTES

TIPS & OPTIONS

I like to keep the skin on my cucumbers for added fiber.

Instamatic Cucumber Salad is the perfect summer barbecue side dish. Pair with any meat from the grill.

Instead of cilantro, try using fresh dill. It makes for a snappy, refreshing alternative.

COUNTDOWN CURRY CHICKEN SALAD

TIPS & OPTIONS ⟫

Interesting fact: The original Waldorf Salad was created in 1893 by Oscar Tschirky, the maître d'hôtel of the Waldorf Astoria in New York City.

Enjoy Countdown Curry Chicken Salad while watching one of my favorite movies filmed at the Waldorf Astoria: *Catch Me If You Can*, *Serendipity*, or *Scent of a Woman*.

Any apple variety will do. Feel free to peel the apple if you prefer.

My twist on the traditional Waldorf salad leaves raisins behind and introduces bright yellow curry to the mix. This combination offers a hint of savory flavor to an already sweet dish, but perhaps more important, it just looks *perty*! Impress your guests by whipping up stunning Countdown Curry Chicken Salad in just 10 minutes flat.

2 Grab and Go Chicken Breasts, cubed (see Chapter 10)

1 cup full-fat mayonnaise

1 cup chopped celery

½ medium Granny Smith apple, cored and chopped

4 ounces chopped walnuts

4 (1-gram) packets 0g net carbs sweetener

1 tablespoon curry powder

1 tablespoon white vinegar

⅛ teaspoon salt

1 (10-ounce) bag prewashed spinach

1 In a medium bowl, combine all ingredients except spinach.

2 Stir to combine and completely coat chicken.

3 Evenly divide spinach among four salad bowls.

4 Top each bowl with one-fourth of chicken curry mix. Cover with wrap and put in refrigerator.

5 Serve chilled.

THAI TIME CRUNCH SALAD

In my "previous life" (when I weighed close to 300 pounds), I frequented Panera Bread for lunch. I ordered the Spicy Thai Salad with Chicken (thinking I was being healthy), a giant Candy Cookie (knowing I wasn't), and washed both down with a Diet Coke (which made up for indiscretions). Little did I know that my meal contained about 100 grams of carbs! That's not even counting the dozen bagels I bought on my way out the door. These days, when I want a fast and casual lunch, I make this Thai Time Crunch Salad.

Dressing

1 tablespoon no-sugar-added peanut butter

1 tablespoon soy sauce

1 tablespoon water

5 (1-gram) packets 0g net carbs sweetener

2 teaspoons apple cider vinegar

⅓ cup sesame oil

⅛ teaspoon ground ginger

½ teaspoon sesame seeds

¼ teaspoon red pepper flakes

¼ cup salted peanuts, crushed

Salad

6 cups shredded cabbage mix (green cabbage, red cabbage, carrot blend)

¼ cup chopped green onion

¼ cup chopped fresh cilantro

1½ cups shredded Grab and Go Chicken Breasts, cold (see Chapter 10)

1　In a medium bowl, whisk together all Dressing ingredients except crushed peanuts. Cover and set aside.

2　In a large mixing bowl, combine cabbage mix, green onion, and cilantro and stir. Add chicken and mix again.

3　Add Dressing to Salad. Toss to fully coat.

4　Divide equally among four bowls. Top with equal amounts of crushed peanuts.

5　Serve chilled.

NET CARBS

5G

SERVES 4

PER SERVING:

CALORIES	323
FAT	24G
PROTEIN	16G
SODIUM	308MG
FIBER	4G
CARBOHYDRATES	9G
NET CARBS	5G
SUGAR	4G

TIME

PREP TIME:	10 MINUTES
COOK TIME:	0 MINUTES
TOTAL TIME:	10 MINUTES

TIPS & OPTIONS

Lettuce can be substituted for the cabbage. A 12-ounce bag (four servings) of pre-washed salad mix will make the job even easier. But don't forget the cilantro! That herb really seals the deal.

For a slightly different twist (not to mention time-saver), reboot leftover Peanut Sauce from the Vietnamese Spring Rolls to Go recipe in Chapter 7, or vice versa, you could reboot the Dressing recipe here to accompany your Vietnamese Spring Rolls to go.

JUST PRESS START "POTATO" SALAD

Potatoes are a food of the past with DIRTY, LAZY, KETO. Even sweet potatoes are crossed off my list! They are both just too starchy for my liking, with 26 and 23 grams of carbs, respectively. Just Press Start "Potato" Salad keeps all the taste of a traditional potato salad, but without unnecessary carbs. That's a win-win in my book!

1 (12-ounce) bag cauliflower florets

3 large eggs, hard-boiled, peeled, and chopped

½ cup chopped celery

½ cup finely chopped red onion

¼ cup full-fat mayonnaise

¼ cup full-fat sour cream

1 tablespoon yellow mustard

½ teaspoon salt

¼ teaspoon ground black pepper

1 In a medium microwave-safe bowl, add cauliflower. Microwave on high 4 minutes. Let cool.

2 Add cauliflower to a large bowl and stir in the remaining ingredients; mix well.

3 Cover and let cool in refrigerator. Serve chilled.

CHAPTER 7

SNACKS

It's almost embarrassing how often I talk about food. When thinking about fast snack ideas to share with you, my mind was flooded with hundreds of helpful tips. Seriously, I had to rein in my excitement! Having DIRTY, LAZY, KETO snacks on hand has been crucial to maintaining my 140-pound weight loss.

> Nibbling on healthy food helps keep the edge off.
> I make better decisions (about everything, really) when
> I'm not feeling so *hangry*.

What makes the perfect DIRTY, LAZY, KETO snack, you ask? I believe snacks should be simple yet filling. That's the whole point, right? Snacks, by design, should get you through the empty transition period in between meals.

If you're like me, when you're hungry, you want something fast. I want a snack to curb a hunger craving without having to do a lot of work. In the past, that meant I reached for mostly unhealthy convenience food like chips or crackers. Unfortunately, those high-carb foods never hit the spot. Since starch, just like sugar, is quickly metabolized by the body, foods like chips and crackers sent my blood sugar levels spiraling out of control. I would end up eating more, not less, making the whole snack experience pointless.

Now my snack options consist of foods with higher amounts of fat, moderate levels of protein, and low carbohydrate numbers. I find DIRTY, LAZY, KETO snacks stop the hunger beast in its tracks. I am able to eat a healthy snack and then move on with my day. You'll notice many of my snack recipes contain vegetables too. The high amount of fiber in slow-burning carbs keeps my metabolism on point. They fill me up and keep me from overeating (which has always been my challenge).

I also drink a lot of water with my snacks. That wouldn't make for a very exciting recipe, but it's worthy of mentioning here! In between meals, I aim to consume as much water as possible. It helps with digestion, keeps me full, and prevents dehydration symptoms (more commonly referred to as the "keto flu").

TURKEY TORRENT MEATBALLS

There is nothing more disappointing than making meatballs that fall apart during cooking. You do so much work to mix and shape the ingredients, only to have a giant crumbly mess in the pan—*frustrating*. Without using bread crumbs as a binder, what's a girl to do? There are plenty of effective DLK options to try. Parmesan cheese, crushed pork rinds, and mozzarella cheese work wonders to maintain the meatball shape. And, as seen in these Turkey Torrent Meatballs, egg and oil also do the trick.

1 pound 85% lean ground turkey

½ (10-ounce) bag frozen riced cauliflower

1 large egg, beaten

1 medium clove garlic, peeled and minced

½ teaspoon ground ginger

¼ teaspoon salt

⅛ teaspoon ground black pepper

1 teaspoon sesame oil

2 tablespoons water

1 In a large bowl, using your hands, combine all ingredients except oil and water. Form fifteen to twenty uniform balls approximately 1" across.

2 In a medium skillet over medium heat, heat oil. Add meatballs and fry 10 minutes, turning regularly, until browned on all sides. Drain any fat from skillet.

3 Add water to skillet and bring to a boil. Reduce heat to low, cover, and simmer 10 minutes.

4 Serve warm.

NET CARBS

1G

SERVES 4

PER SERVING:

CALORIES	286
FAT	17G
PROTEIN	27G
SODIUM	253MG
FIBER	1G
CARBOHYDRATES	2G
NET CARBS	1G
SUGAR	1G

TIME

PREP TIME:	10 MINUTES
COOK TIME:	20 MINUTES
TOTAL TIME:	30 MINUTES

TIPS & OPTIONS

When it comes to flavor, fat matters. Choose 85% lean ground turkey for a much better taste than the rubbery, low-fat variety.

Serve with Asian stir-fry veggies like bok choy, bean sprouts, mushrooms, and bamboo shoots.

Chopsticks make a meal special. Even the most un-coordinated family members can stab a meatball with their sticks!

AGILE "APPLE" CRISP

TIPS & OPTIONS

Chayotes come in two forms: prickly and smooth.

If you want a stronger apple taste, add 2 teaspoons apple extract or mix in a peeled, cored, and diced medium Granny Smith apple with the chayote (for an increase of 4–5 net carbs per serving).

It's not just the fruit of the chayote plant that's edible. You can eat the tendrils and flowers from the vine too!

Years ago, we moved into a house with a suspicious vine overtaking the front yard. I woke up every morning to find the spiky vine had grown at least another foot, like I was in some kind of twisted "Jack and the Beanstalk" story. Little did I know this was a producing chayote plant. With a bushel of this low-carb fruit at my disposal (4g net carbs per cup), I started getting creative in the kitchen. We ate a lot of chayote that year! Agile "Apple" Crisp was the champion recipe of the season.

Almond Crumble

¾ cup superfine blanched almond flour

5 tablespoons 0g net carbs sweetener

2 tablespoons coconut flour

½ teaspoon ground cinnamon

⅛ teaspoon salt

¼ cup cold unsalted butter, cubed

Chayote Filling

4 large chayotes, peeled, cored, and diced

¼ cup unsalted butter, melted

3 tablespoons 0g net carbs sweetener

3 tablespoons 100% lemon juice

1 teaspoon ground cinnamon

½ teaspoon ground nutmeg

¼ teaspoon ground allspice

1 Preheat oven to 375°F. Grease a 9" × 7" baking dish.

2 In a medium nonstick skillet over medium heat, add almond flour. Toast almond flour 3 minutes while stirring.

3 In a medium bowl, combine toasted almond flour, sweetener, coconut flour, cinnamon, and salt. Stir to combine well.

4 Using two knives or a pastry blender, cut in butter until the mixture resembles coarse crumbs and butter is fully incorporated.

5 Add all Chayote Filling ingredients to prepared baking dish. Stir to combine and coat completely.

6 Top with even layer of Almond Crumble and bake 15–20 minutes covered until cooked throughout. Serve warm.

FLY OFF THE PLATE ROOSTER WINGS

Wings are the perfect pizza alternative at my house. Every Friday night, my kids insist on eating Little Caesars pizza. If I want a night off from the kitchen, I'll tack on a request for wings to their order. It's not hard to make my own, though. Ironically, it's faster too! My plate of Fly Off the Plate Rooster Wings is ready in less time than it takes to jet across town and back with takeout.

> 6 ounces (approximately 4–6) chicken wing sections, drumette or "flat"
>
> 2 tablespoons olive oil, divided
>
> 1 tablespoon baking powder
>
> 1 teaspoon ground fresh chili paste
>
> ¼ teaspoon salt
>
> 1 medium clove garlic, peeled and minced
>
> 2 tablespoons rebooted DLK House Ranch Dressing (see Hurry Up House Salad with Ranch in Chapter 6)

1   Preheat air fryer to 400°F.

2   On a medium plate, brush chicken wings with 1 tablespoon oil. Generously sprinkle both sides of wings with baking powder.

3   Spread out wings on crisper tray. Cook in air fryer 15–20 minutes, tossing once halfway through until dry and golden.

4   In a medium bowl, whisk to combine remaining 1 tablespoon oil, chili paste, salt, and garlic.

5   Add cooked wings to sauce mixture and toss until completely coated.

6   Serve warm with DLK House Ranch Dressing in a dipping bowl on the side.

NET CARBS
6G

SERVES 1

PER SERVING:

CALORIES	663
FAT	57G
PROTEIN	30G
SODIUM	2,373MG
FIBER	0G
CARBOHYDRATES	6G
NET CARBS	6G
SUGAR	1G

TIME

PREP TIME:	5 MINUTES
COOK TIME:	20 MINUTES
TOTAL TIME:	25 MINUTES

TIPS & OPTIONS

Anyone who has perused the DIRTY, LAZY, KETO cookbooks knows about my husband's love affair with the "rooster" chili paste called Sambal Oelek, made by Huy Fong Foods. (It has the famous fowl as its logo.) He puts it on almost everything he eats, including wings.

The wings should only be lightly coated in sauce, just enough to give them flavor.

Serve wings with celery stalks, ranch dressing, and lots of napkins!

VIETNAMESE SPRING ROLLS TO GO

In truth, spring rolls are just a vehicle for me to eat more peanut sauce. I could probably eat this peanut sauce every day—no exaggeration—because I love it so much. It deserves a DIRTY, LAZY, KETO gold star! For me, it's like the ranch dressing of Vietnamese food. Use fat to make healthy food taste better, right?

4 cups water

4 outer leaves from medium head green cabbage, trimmed

4 (1-gram) packets 0g net carbs sweetener

½ teaspoon sesame seeds

Peanut Sauce

⅓ cup no-sugar-added creamy peanut butter, softened

1½ tablespoons water

1 tablespoon soy sauce

½ tablespoon 100% lime juice

1 teaspoon white vinegar

1 teaspoon ground ginger

1 medium clove garlic, peeled and minced

Filling

½ cup mung bean sprouts

½ cup shredded cabbage

½ cup shredded cucumber

½ medium avocado, peeled, pitted, and thinly sliced

¼ cup finely chopped green onion

1 tablespoon chopped fresh cilantro

TIPS & OPTIONS

Give the sauce some kick by adding sriracha sauce and red pepper flakes.

Add 1 teaspoon crushed peanuts to the sauce for more texture.

To save on carb count, try using powdered peanut butter (3g net carbs per 2-tablespoon serving). I've been experimenting with great success using Simply Nature Organic Peanut Butter Powder.

1   Boil water in a large saucepan. Carefully add cabbage leaves to boiling water. Boil cabbage 2 minutes, stirring and rearranging leaves using metal tongs to cook evenly.

2   Drain cabbage and cool leaves by running cold tap water into saucepan.

3   In a small microwave-safe bowl, whisk all Peanut Sauce ingredients until mixed and sweetener is dissolved. If peanut butter is stiff, microwave covered sauce 10–20 seconds until softened and whisk again. Evenly divide sauce among four small serving bowls.

4   Put 1 cabbage leaf on each of four dinner plates.

5   On one half near the center, top each leaf evenly with one-fourth of each of the Filling ingredients.

6   Roll up each cabbage leaf like a burrito into a spring roll.

7   Serve immediately with Peanut Sauce.

SUPERSONIC SUSHI-STYLE ROLLS

Japanese restaurants can be intimidating when you're eating low carb. Every dish seems to come with rice! Look closer at the menu, however, and you'll notice there are many more options beyond the traditional sushi roll. Edamame, sashimi, and ahi salad are part of my standing order, but you may also consider yakiniku (boneless short rib), yakitori (skewered chicken), wakame sarada (seaweed salad), or miso soup. If I'm really craving a true sushi roll, I make my own using thinly sliced cucumber or seaweed as a wrap.

1 (10-ounce) bag frozen riced cauliflower

2 tablespoons full-fat cream cheese, softened

2 teaspoons sesame oil

¼ teaspoon salt

2 sheets sushi nori seaweed, 7½" × 8½" each

¼ pound raw salmon steak (no skin), thinly sliced

½ cup matchstick-sliced cucumber

½ cup matchstick-sliced red bell pepper

½ medium avocado, peeled, pitted, and thinly sliced

1 tablespoon toasted sesame seeds

1   In a medium microwave-safe bowl, add cauliflower and microwave on high 4–5 minutes until tender. Let cool and place on clean kitchen towel. Wrap up cauliflower and squeeze out any excess water.

2   Return to bowl and mix in cream cheese, sesame oil, and salt.

3   Lay out a large piece of plastic wrap on counter. Place two pieces mostly square seaweed on plastic wrap, side by side, and moisten with water.

4   Evenly spread a thin layer (about ¼") cauliflower mixture on both sheets of seaweed.

5   Next, evenly spread salmon, cucumber, bell pepper, avocado, and sesame seeds on cauliflower mixture.

6   Starting at the side closest to you, slowly roll each seaweed sheet. If parts of seaweed are dry and brittle, brush with water. Cut each roll in half and refrigerate covered.

7   Place one 4" roll on each of four plates. Serve.

NET CARBS
4G

SERVES 4

PER SERVING:

CALORIES	180
FAT	12G
PROTEIN	9G
SODIUM	204MG
FIBER	4G
CARBOHYDRATES	8G
NET CARBS	4G
SUGAR	3G

TIME

PREP TIME:	15 MINUTES
COOK TIME:	5 MINUTES
TOTAL TIME:	20 MINUTES

TIPS & OPTIONS

For best results, start the rolling process at the edge closest to you (lift the edge of the plastic wrap to get it started).

Your roll should only overlap the opposite side by ¼"–½" (which helps seal the roll closed).

Serve with soy sauce and wasabi.

Roasted seaweed snacks have become all the rage with millennials. Instead of salty chips, be one of the cool kids and munch on a snack pack of nori seaweed chips.

NIMBLE "NACHOS"

TIPS & OPTIONS

Optional toppings are diced tomato, sour cream, sliced olives, and chunks of avocado.

Nachos are best enjoyed while sipping a low-carb beer. Some of my favorites are Corona Premier, Michelob Ultra, or Miller Lite (all have 3 grams net carbs per 12-ounce serving).

In a hurry? Make "chips" in the air fryer. Brush low-carb tortillas with oil and salt, cut into triangles, and bake 4–6 minutes at 400°F until crispy, stopping every couple of minutes to shake the basket.

Eating nachos and losing weight? I'm determined to revise and revive old favorites in a new, healthier way. Nachos are just one example.

"Tortilla" Chips

2 cups riced cauliflower

1 cup grated Parmesan cheese

1 teaspoon DLK House Ranch Dressing Mix (see Hurry Up House Salad with Ranch in Chapter 6)

⅛ teaspoon salt

⅛ teaspoon ground black pepper

Cheese Sauce

1½ cups shredded Cheddar cheese

¼ cup full-fat cream cheese, softened

¼ cup unsweetened almond milk

½ teaspoon ground cumin

½ teaspoon salt

½ teaspoon chili powder

Toppings

1 small jalapeño pepper, steamed, seeded, deveined, and thinly sliced into rings

½ tablespoon chopped fresh cilantro

1 Preheat oven to 375°F.

2 In a medium microwave-safe bowl, add cauliflower and microwave on high 4–5 minutes until tender. Let cool and place on a clean kitchen towel. Wrap up cauliflower and squeeze out any excess water.

3 Return to bowl and add Parmesan, DLK House Ranch Dressing Mix, salt, and pepper. Mix until a moist dough is formed.

4 Place dough on a large piece of parchment paper and place a second piece of paper on top of dough. Use a rolling pin to flatten dough to the thickness of a Dorito.

5 Remove top piece of paper. Use a pizza cutter to cut dough into triangles, roughly the size of Doritos.

6 Transfer parchment paper with chips on it to a large baking sheet.

7 Bake 15 minutes until golden brown.

8 In a medium microwave-safe bowl, combine all Cheese Sauce ingredients. Microwave on high 30 seconds. Stir and microwave another 30 seconds until smooth.

9 Put all chips in a medium decorative bowl and top with Cheese Sauce. Garnish with jalapeño slices and cilantro.

CLIP CHIPS AND SALSA

Are you an experienced diner? (Don't laugh, but I once heard that question posed during a hotel room TV infomercial in Las Vegas.) Seriously, though, my advanced palate should be awarded a Michelin star for its ability to discern among junk food flavors. Diet Pepsi versus Diet Coke? That's too easy. McDonald's fries versus Burger King fries? Amateur hour. Give me a real challenge. Let's talk about chips! I can discern the subtle nuances among tortilla chips served at every chain restaurant, with Clip Chips and Salsa being my favorite (and from my own kitchen!).

NET CARBS

10G

SERVES 4

PER SERVING:
CALORIES	182
FAT	12G
PROTEIN	6G
SODIUM	727MG
FIBER	14G
CARBOHYDRATES	24G
NET CARBS	10G
SUGAR	5G

TIME

PREP TIME:	10 MINUTES
COOK TIME:	15 MINUTES
TOTAL TIME:	25 MINUTES

TIPS & OPTIONS ⟫

No time to make your own salsa? Take a shortcut today and buy a jar of La Victoria Thick 'n Chunky Salsa Verde Medium (6 grams net carbs per ¾-cup serving). I won't tell anyone your salsa is not homemade.

In general, green salsa (verde) is lower in net carbs compared to red salsa.

Resist the temptation to blend the Salsa Verde too long, creating a lifeless soup. A little texture/lumpiness gives it character.

Chips

3 tablespoons olive oil

1 tablespoon 100% lime juice

½ teaspoon chili powder

½ teaspoon ground cumin

⅛ teaspoon garlic powder

¼ teaspoon paprika

½ teaspoon salt

4 low-carb flour tortillas or reboot Tempo Tortillas (see Chapter 8)

Salsa Verde

1 pound medium tomatillos, peeled, stemmed, and quartered

2 medium jalapeño peppers, seeded, deveined, and minced

¼ medium yellow onion, peeled and minced

2 teaspoons minced garlic

1 tablespoon 100% lime juice

¼ cup chopped fresh cilantro

¼ teaspoon salt

⅛ teaspoon ground black pepper

⅛ teaspoon ground cumin

1   Preheat oven to 425°F. Line a baking sheet with parchment paper.

2   In a small bowl, whisk to combine oil and lime juice.

3   In a separate small bowl, whisk to combine remaining Chips ingredients except tortillas.

4   Using a basting brush, coat both sides of four tortillas with oil mixture.

5   Evenly dust both sides of moistened tortillas with chili powder mixture.

6   Using a pizza cutter, slice tortillas into eight triangles.

7　Evenly distribute tortilla slices on prepared baking sheet without touching. Bake until crunchy, 8–10 minutes, flipping chips over halfway through.

8　Preheat broiler to high. Cover a baking sheet with greased foil.

9　Place tomatillos, jalapeños, onion, and garlic on prepared baking sheet and broil on high 4–5 minutes, stirring every minute until starting to char.

10　In a food processor, add roasted vegetables and remaining Salsa Verde ingredients. Pulse 30–60 seconds until desired consistency is achieved.

11　Pour Salsa Verde into a small decorative dipping bowl.

12　Transfer chips to a large decorative platter and serve with bowl of Salsa Verde in the center.

CLOSE THE KITCHEN EARLY QUESADILLAS

A rotisserie chicken is a weekly staple on my shopping list. Every grocery store in my community sells these precooked beauties, all at a similar, reasonable price point. I want to remove any potential excuses that might pop up about cooking dinner. Rotisserie chickens are such a time-saver! Having precooked chicken at my fingertips makes it easy to whip up meals like Close the Kitchen Early Quesadillas.

Barbecue Sauce

⅔ cup no-sugar-added ketchup

1 tablespoon olive oil

1 tablespoon white vinegar

1 tablespoon 100% lemon juice

½ teaspoon minced garlic

1 teaspoon paprika

½ teaspoon ground chili powder

¼ teaspoon salt

2 (1-gram) packets 0g net carbs sweetener

⅛ teaspoon xanthan gum

Chicken Quesadillas

2 cups cooked and shredded chicken (from rotisserie)

1 cup shredded Cheddar cheese

¼ cup chopped green onion

4 (8") low-carb flour tortillas

2 tablespoons unsalted butter

½ cup full-fat sour cream

2 tablespoons chopped fresh cilantro

1   In a large skillet over medium heat, heat all Barbecue Sauce ingredients 10 minutes, stirring regularly to thicken. Sprinkle in xanthan gum slowly to prevent clumping.

2   Fold in chicken, Cheddar, and onion until combined.

3   Divide mixture evenly among four tortillas on four dinner plates. Place mixture evenly on one half of each tortilla and fold in half.

4   In a large skillet over medium heat, melt butter. Add two quesadillas to the skillet and fry 2 minutes until golden. Flip and cook another 2 minutes. Repeat for second batch and transfer to dinner plates.

5   Top each quesadilla evenly with a dollop of sour cream and chopped cilantro. Serve warm.

NET CARBS
8G

SERVES 4

PER SERVING:

CALORIES	435
FAT	26G
PROTEIN	34G
SODIUM	1,190MG
FIBER	12G
CARBOHYDRATES	20G
NET CARBS	8G
SUGAR	4G

TIME	
PREP TIME:	10 MINUTES
COOK TIME:	18 MINUTES
TOTAL TIME:	28 MINUTES

TIPS & OPTIONS

Try using the brand Olé Mexican Foods Xtreme Wellness! Tortilla Wraps, which have 5 grams net carbs per tortilla.

In a hurry? Skip a step by using store-bought G Hughes Sugar Free BBQ Sauce (available in Honey, Hickory, Sweet & Spicy, Mesquite, Maple Brown, Carolina Style Sweet Heat, or Original flavors).

As a side dish, heat up a can of low-carb Eden Organic Black Soy Beans (available online) at 1 gram net carbs per ½-cup serving.

Instead of buying a rotisserie chicken, reboot Grab and Go Chicken Breasts (see Chapter 10) here.

HIGH-SPEED SAUSAGE BITES

TIPS & OPTIONS »

Bring a platter of High-Speed Sausage Bites to your next get-together. Serve with decorative toothpicks in lieu of silverware.

Don't have a waffle maker? Heat sausage bites on an outdoor grill or in a skillet (filled with a small amount of water) on the stovetop.

I prefer Aidells brand of smoked sausages. Some of my favorite smoked chicken flavors include Chicken & Apple and Artichoke & Garlic. For smoked pork sausage, I recommend the Aidells Cajun Style Andouille.

I'm always on the lookout for creative ways to maximize the efficiency of my counter space. Kitchen appliances, in particular, are one of my sore spots. They take up too much room! In order to claim a permanent spot on my limited real estate, a gadget must multitask. I was about to relocate my waffle maker to a "weekend only" cabinet when it hit me: I could use this gadget to heat up sausages for tonight's dinner, George Foreman–style! High-Speed Sausage Bites (with minimal prep and execution) are ready in seconds flat.

> 2 tablespoons full-fat mayonnaise
>
> ½ tablespoon yellow mustard
>
> 1 teaspoon sriracha
>
> 1 teaspoon minced garlic
>
> ⅛ teaspoon ground paprika
>
> ⅛ teaspoon salt
>
> ⅛ teaspoon ground black pepper
>
> 1 (12-ounce) package low-carb precooked chicken sausage links, sliced lengthwise in half and then into ½"–¾" pieces

1 Grease a waffle maker with nonstick cooking spray and preheat.

2 In a medium bowl, whisk together all ingredients except sausage bites until well blended.

3 Working in batches, distribute sausage bites on waffle maker and close. Cook 3 minutes. Repeat process until all sausages are cooked.

4 Add hot sausage bites to bowl with sauce and toss to coat.

5 Serve warm in four medium fancy bowls.

CONVENIENT CHILI-CHEESE DOGS

Dirty Keto catches a lot of heat in the media. Critics think we're just eating bunless, triple-bacon burgers from the drive-thru on our way to shop for skinny pants. This couldn't be further from the truth (well, maybe keep the skinny pants part). In reality, the "dirty" part of DIRTY, LAZY, KETO means we are open-minded with ingredient choices. Don't confuse that with eating low-quality foods 24/7! Instead, it's about flexible options. I can have a Convenient Chili-Cheese Dog with a side of organic vegetables if I want to—*nothing is off limits*.

NET CARBS	
10G	

SERVES 4	
PER SERVING:	
CALORIES	578
FAT	31G
PROTEIN	44G
SODIUM	1,294MG
FIBER	10G
CARBOHYDRATES	20G
NET CARBS	10G
SUGAR	5G

TIME	
PREP TIME:	5 MINUTES
COOK TIME:	22 MINUTES
TOTAL TIME:	27 MINUTES

Chili

1 pound 90% lean ground beef

½ cup diced yellow onion

1 teaspoon minced garlic

1 (1.25-ounce) packet chili seasoning mix

1 (14.5-ounce) can no-sugar-added diced tomatoes, undrained

1 (15-ounce) can no-salt-added black soybeans, undrained

¼ teaspoon salt

Cheese Dogs

4 beef hot dogs

4 (19-gram) slices Cheddar cheese

1. In a medium nonstick skillet over medium heat, add beef, onion, and garlic. Cook 10–15 minutes while stirring until beef is no longer pink. Drain fat.

2. Add remaining Chili Ingredients to skillet and cook 5 more minutes while stirring.

3. On a medium microwave-safe plate, place all 4 hot dogs and microwave on high 1½ minutes.

4. Using tongs, place each hot dog on a separate plate and top each with 1 slice Cheddar.

5. Top each cheese-covered dog with ¼ cup hot Chili.

6. Serve warm.

TIPS & OPTIONS

Don't worry about over-microwaving the hot dogs and having them split. No one will notice! The cheese and chili will hide any accidents.

In a hurry? Use chili from a can! A popular low-carb brand is Skyline Original Chili with 2 grams net carbs per cup.

Reboot extra servings of Gassed-Up Chili (see Chapter 6) in this recipe.

Black soybeans are a relatively new phenomenon. I buy Eden Organic Black Soy Beans with no salt added in 15-ounce can online. Miraculously, they have only 1 gram net carbs per ½-cup serving and 3.5 grams net carbs per 15-ounce can.

DEADLINE DEVILED AVOCADOS

NET CARBS

2G

SERVES 4

PER SERVING:

CALORIES	140
FAT	12G
PROTEIN	1G
SODIUM	224MG
FIBER	5G
CARBOHYDRATES	7G
NET CARBS	2G
SUGAR	1G

TIME

PREP TIME:	10 MINUTES
COOK TIME:	0 MINUTES
TOTAL TIME:	10 MINUTES

TIPS & OPTIONS »

Catch a sale on a bag of mini avocados? Make a whole platter of Deadline Deviled Avocados for an appetizer.

For variety, add cold baby shrimp as a topper.

Presentation is everything, right? These Deadline Deviled Avocados are so darn cute. I love food served in surprising ways! Bring a platter of these to your next party or serve for a ladies' luncheon and you'll be certain to get a boatload of compliments. Eating healthy doesn't have to be boring. Dress up your plate, even if it's just to impress yourself. You're worth the effort!

2 large avocados, halved and pitted (leave the skin on)
1 tablespoon full-fat mayonnaise
½ tablespoon 100% lemon juice
1 tablespoon sriracha sauce
¼ teaspoon garlic salt
⅛ teaspoon ground black pepper
⅛ teaspoon ground paprika

1 For each avocado half, carefully scrape out about half of the avocado flesh from the center, leaving a thick border all the way around the shell. Transfer scooped-out avocado flesh to a medium bowl.

2 Thoroughly mash avocado and mix in remaining ingredients, except paprika, until combined.

3 Divide mixture evenly among avocado halves and top with sprinkle of paprika.

4 Cover and put in refrigerator. Serve chilled.

STEP ON IT PICKLE STACKERS

Commercial cheese-and-egg wraps are all the rage these days. These quick substitutions for sandwich making are tempting for newbies who are still in mourning over cutting bread from their diet. Personally, I find these substitutions hard to find and often expensive. Wrapping my "sandwich" in lettuce leaves, sliced deli meat, or even pickles as shown here, is just as effective (and novel). And it saves me a trip to the store.

1 pound deli-sliced turkey breast

¼ cup full-fat mayonnaise

2 teaspoons yellow mustard

2 strips no-sugar-added bacon, cooked and crumbled

2 cups shredded iceberg lettuce

½ cup chopped tomato

¼ cup finely sliced red onion

½ cup shredded Cheddar cheese

2 large whole dill pickles

1   Divide turkey evenly into four portions and arrange on plates. If multiple slices are on a plate, organize so they form a circle no more than 4"–5" across and are an even thickness as much as possible.

2   In a small bowl, combine mayonnaise and mustard. Spread evenly on turkey wrappers.

3   Evenly layer all remaining ingredients, except pickles, on turkey slices.

4   Roll each turkey deli wrap.

5   Slice each pickle lengthwise into four long, flat slices each (eight slices total). These will serve as the "buns."

6   Insert each turkey deli wrap inside a pair of pickle slices. Secure with toothpick. Cover and put in refrigerator.

7   Serve chilled.

NET CARBS

7G

SERVES 4

PER SERVING:

CALORIES	312
FAT	18G
PROTEIN	26G
SODIUM	1,948MG
FIBER	2G
CARBOHYDRATES	9G
NET CARBS	7G
SUGAR	4G

TIME

PREP TIME:	10 MINUTES
COOK TIME:	0 MINUTES
TOTAL TIME:	10 MINUTES

TIPS & OPTIONS

Adjust mayonnaise and mustard amounts to your particular tastes.

Instead of mustard, substitute a spoonful of pesto. When mixed with the mayonnaise, this creates a delightful zing! I buy a jar of fresh pesto every time I visit Costco—the competitive price on this pesto beats buying the required ingredients to make fresh pesto at home.

SPEEDY SEVEN-LAYER DIP

NET CARBS

4G

SERVES 6

PER SERVING:
CALORIES   219
FAT   12G
PROTEIN   19G
SODIUM   224MG
FIBER   0G
CARBOHYDRATES   4G
NET CARBS   4G
SUGAR   2G

TIME

PREP TIME: 10 MINUTES
COOK TIME: 15 MINUTES
TOTAL TIME: 25 MINUTES

TIPS & OPTIONS »

Suggested toppings are cilantro, avocado, and jalapeño rings.

Scoop this dip with my very own Clip Chips and Salsa recipe in this chapter.

Serve with a platter of hearty fresh veggies for dipping, like cauliflower florets or bell pepper slices. Better yet? Bring a plastic spoon. No one likes double-dippers!

I always bring a dish to parties, even when I'm not asked. First of all, I think bringing a gift is a nice thing to do, but more important, I want to make sure I have something low-carb to eat. Sure, what I bring depends on the type of get-together, but I find a casual dish like Speedy Seven-Layer Dip goes well with whatever the person is planning.

1 pound 93% lean ground beef

1 tablespoon taco seasoning

¾ cup full-fat sour cream

½ cup shredded iceberg lettuce

½ cup shredded Mexican-style cheese blend

½ cup diced tomato

2 tablespoons chopped green onion

2 tablespoons diced black olives

½ cup no-sugar-added salsa

1 Grease a 9" × 9" × 2" baking dish and set aside.

2 In a medium skillet over medium heat, cook beef 10 minutes while stirring.

3 Stir in taco seasoning and cook 5 more minutes.

4 Evenly spread meat in prepared baking dish.

5 Next, in this order, layer sour cream, lettuce, cheese, tomato, onion, olives, and salsa.

6 Cover and put in refrigerator until ready to serve. Serve chilled.

CHAPTER 8

BREADS AND PIZZA

Raise your hand if you have a bread-making machine somewhere in the bowels of your kitchen. Anyone, *anyone?* You're not alone. I too was brought up with the false belief that if I ate bread that was homemade—or even better, made with whole wheat—I was on my way to picture-perfect health. Boy, was I wrong! …*on all counts*.

As it turns out, for many of us, bread of any kind causes more harm to our health than good. (At least that's been my experience.) Interestingly, despite knowing how many carbs are in each serving of bread, many people struggle finding a satisfactory alternative. They become stuck before even starting DIRTY, LAZY, KETO.

"How do you make a sandwich?" they ponder.

"What about pizza?" they question.

"How do you hold a hot dog?" and so on, and so forth.

I empathize. Cutting out long-standing traditions like morning toast or a PB&J sandwich seems downright *un-American*. I agree! But what if there is another way? One of the reasons I've been so successful in maintaining my 140-pound weight loss *for eight years* is that I've fully embraced cheap, easy, and tasty bread-swap options.

Instead of buying overpriced loaves of "cardboard" from the Internet, I make my own tasty rolls, crackers, and breads. I don't buy expensive "keto" pizza crusts; I create a low-carb version at home. I don't feel deprived, because I'm not missing out! I continue to cook and eat "normal foods" just like everybody else.

I will admit, however, that my bread habits have evolved over time. I've learned to swap out some breads altogether for my *new* favorites. For lunch, I enjoy an *unwich* wrapped in lettuce. My favorite pizza crust is now made from chicken! These substitutes taste delicious. In fact, I love these breadless versions even more than their original. By becoming open-minded and taking risks to try familiar favorites in a new way, I've created my own *new normal* with DIRTY, LAZY, KETO. Be brave and come join me!

PROCRASTINATOR PIZZA CASSEROLE

You can tell a lot about a person by peeking into their freezer. Mine is overstocked (some might say "crammed") with the most unusual items. Call me overprepared, but if a pizza hankering comes on, I won't be calling for delivery.

Crust

2 (10-ounce) bags frozen riced cauliflower

1 large egg, beaten

¾ cup shredded Cheddar cheese, softened

1 medium clove garlic, peeled and minced

1½ teaspoons Italian seasoning

¼ teaspoon salt

⅛ teaspoon ground black pepper

Toppings

1 cup no-sugar-added pasta sauce

1 teaspoon Italian seasoning

1 medium clove garlic, peeled and minced

¼ teaspoon salt

2 cups shredded whole milk mozzarella cheese

8 slices pepperoni

1 teaspoon dried parsley

1 Preheat oven to 420°F. Grease a 9" × 9" baking dish.

2 In a medium microwave-safe bowl, add cauliflower and microwave on high 4–5 minutes until tender. Let cool and place on a clean kitchen towel. Wrap up cauliflower and squeeze out any excess water.

3 In a large bowl, combine cauliflower with remaining Crust ingredients. Stir until dough forms.

4 Place dough ball in prepared baking dish. Using your hands, spread the dough evenly, pushing firmly into place (dough will be somewhat loose).

5 Bake 8–10 minutes until crust is golden and crispy. If crust overbrowns too early, cover with foil and return to oven.

6 In a medium bowl, whisk together pasta sauce, Italian seasoning, garlic, and salt until well blended.

7 Remove crust from oven and evenly spread sauce mixture on top. Next, evenly top with mozzarella. Finally, top evenly with pepperoni slices.

8 Return to oven 3–5 minutes to melt cheese.

9 Cut into six slices, sprinkle evenly with parsley, and serve.

TIPS & OPTIONS

Quickly drain cauliflower mixture by "smooshing" (that's a technical kitchen word, by the way) it in a fine-mesh strainer using a spatula, repeatedly pressing down to eliminate remaining moisture.

I like to sneak vegetable toppings onto my pizza. Whether I want them there or not isn't the issue—the added fiber and overall "healthiness" helps prevent me from overeating too many slices.

Some of my favorite low-carb pizza toppings include sliced mushrooms, broccoli, black olives, green bell pepper, zucchini, and spinach.

TICK TACO PIZZA

NET CARBS

5G

SERVES 6

PER SERVING:

CALORIES	452
FAT	27G
PROTEIN	39G
SODIUM	797MG
FIBER	1G
CARBOHYDRATES	6G
NET CARBS	5G
SUGAR	2G

TIME

PREP TIME:	10 MINUTES
COOK TIME:	20 MINUTES
TOTAL TIME:	30 MINUTES

TIPS & OPTIONS

If you're using jalapeños from a can or jar then there is no need to remove the seeds. The pickling process removes some of the heat.

After the final baking step (and pizza has cooled down enough to eat), you can top your slice with fresh lettuce, tomatoes, and onions. *Build it like its namesake, the taco!*

Don't be shy. Enjoy salsa, sour cream, or sliced avocado with your meal.

The two dinners my family can agree on are pizza and tacos. One day I figured, why not have them both at the same time? This fun twist on traditional favorites is executed quickly and sure to please even the pickiest of eaters at your dinner table.

Crust

5 large eggs, beaten

2 cups shredded whole milk mozzarella cheese

Toppings

3 tablespoons no-sugar-added tomato paste

1 tablespoon taco seasoning

2 cups shredded Cheddar cheese

1 recipe Ready, Set, Go Ground Beef (see Chapter 10)

½ cup diced red onion

¼ cup thinly sliced jalapeño peppers

1 Preheat oven to 400°F. Line a round 16" pizza pan with parchment paper.

2 In a medium bowl, add eggs and mozzarella. Stir to combine thoroughly.

3 Spread batter on pizza pan in the shape of a circle approximately ¼" thick.

4 Bake 15 minutes until crust is golden and firm. Let cool.

5 Raise oven temperature to 450°F.

6 In a small bowl, combine tomato paste and taco seasoning. Spread mixture evenly on crust.

7 Evenly spread Cheddar; Ready, Set, Go Ground Beef; onion; and jalapeños (in that order) on crust.

8 Bake 5 minutes until cheese is melted and vegetables are soft.

9 Cut into six pieces and serve warm.

MARGHERITA PRONTO PIZZA

When I was younger, I thought there was something wrong with Margherita-style pizza. "What's the deal with the giant white globs of cheese?" I wondered, thinking someone had made a mistake. It wasn't until adulthood that I began to appreciate the subtle nuances of different pizza styles. Made in a new lower-carb fashion, Margherita Pronto Pizza continues to be one of my favorites.

Crust

1 cup superfine blanched almond flour

2 cups shredded whole milk mozzarella cheese

2 tablespoons full-fat cream cheese

1 large egg, beaten

¼ teaspoon salt

Toppings

⅓ cup no-sugar-added tomato sauce

2 teaspoons Italian seasoning

3 (21-gram) slices whole milk mozzarella cheese, broken into 1"–2" circular pieces

1 tablespoon chopped fresh basil

1. Preheat oven to 425°F. Line an ungreased 16" round pizza pan with parchment paper.

2. In a large microwave-safe bowl, combine almond flour, mozzarella, and cream cheese. Microwave on high 1 minute. Stir and microwave another 30 seconds.

3. Fold in egg and salt until dough forms.

4. Put dough on pizza pan and flatten in a circular shape to no more than ¼" thickness.

5. Bake 7–10 minutes until top begins to brown. Remove from oven.

6. In a small bowl, combine tomato sauce and Italian seasoning. Mix well. Evenly spread sauce on crust. Evenly distribute mozzarella pieces over top.

7. Return to oven and bake 5 minutes to melt cheese.

8. Top with fresh basil. Using a pizza cutter, cut into six even slices. Serve warm.

NET CARBS
4G

SERVES 6

PER SERVING:

CALORIES	294
FAT	22G
PROTEIN	16G
SODIUM	505MG
FIBER	2G
CARBOHYDRATES	6G
NET CARBS	4G
SUGAR	2G

TIME

PREP TIME:	10 MINUTES
COOK TIME:	16 MINUTES, 30 SECONDS
TOTAL TIME:	26 MINUTES, 30 SECONDS

TIPS & OPTIONS

Serve with grated Parmesan, garlic, or red pepper flakes.

Instead of chopping the fresh basil, cut the leaves into ribbons. Tightly roll a handful of fresh basil leaves (into a shape like a pencil) and slice every ⅛" or so. The leaves unroll into elegant ribbons for you to top the pizza with. *Fancy, right?*

PORTOBELLO PACED PIZZA

TIPS & OPTIONS 》

If you partially cover the vegetables with a little cheese prior to baking, they cook faster.

Sprinkle red pepper flakes, if desired, on top prior to serving.

Mushrooms contain a lot of water. By slightly elevating them on a baking rack (also called a roasting rack) during the cooking process, you avoid the dreaded soggy-bottom pizza crust.

Ladies and gentlemen, we have to broaden what we think of as pizza if this is going to work. En Vogue reminds me, "Free your mind and the rest will follow" (from one of my favorite 1992 songs, "Free Your Mind"). If that helps, sing along. Let the creativity flow when it comes to pizza. No, that's not a slice of deep-dish pizza on your plate; it's a Portobello Paced Pizza created from a giant mushroom cap. *No joke.*

1 cup no-sugar-added pasta sauce

1 tablespoon Italian seasoning

1 medium clove garlic, peeled and minced

¼ teaspoon salt, divided

4 large portobello mushroom caps

2 tablespoons olive oil

1 cup shredded whole milk mozzarella cheese

¼ cup sliced black olives

¼ cup sliced red bell pepper

2 tablespoons grated Parmesan cheese

1　Preheat oven to 425°F. Grease a 9" × 12" × 2" baking dish. Place a baking rack inside.

2　In a medium bowl, whisk together pasta sauce, Italian seasoning, garlic, and ⅛ teaspoon salt.

3　Scrape black gills out of each mushroom cap and rinse. Pat dry and brush top (round part) of each cap with a heavy coating of oil. Sprinkle oil-coated cap (round side) with remaining salt.

4　Place caps on baking rack in baking dish, gill side up, and evenly fill each with one-fourth of sauce mixture.

5　Divide mozzarella evenly among four caps and top with olives and bell peppers. Dust with Parmesan.

6　Bake 15–20 minutes until caps are softened throughout and cheese is melted. Cover with foil halfway through when browning starts.

7　Serve warm.

GO GO GRILLED CHEESE

There are a handful of meals that people commonly mourn when starting DIRTY, LAZY, KETO. For some reason, grilled cheese is one of them. I'm not sure if it's due to nostalgia or taste, but people love this sandwich! For all those guys and gals, this one's for you.

2 large eggs, beaten

¼ cup full-fat mayonnaise

1 cup crushed pork rinds

1 cup shredded whole milk mozzarella cheese

½ cup shredded Cheddar cheese, divided

1 In a medium bowl, whisk to combine eggs and mayonnaise. Fold in pork rinds and mozzarella to form dough.

2 Divide dough into four even balls. Form each dough ball into a flat patty ¼"–½" thick.

3 Heat a large nonstick skillet over medium heat.

4 Cook two patties at a time in the skillet 3–5 minutes until bottom is golden. Flip both and top one with ¼ cup Cheddar. Cook 3–5 minutes until firm and bottoms are golden.

5 Remove to a plate and top cheese-covered bun with bun top (hot side down to continue melting cheese).

6 Repeat for second Go Go Grilled Cheese. Serve warm.

NET CARBS
2G

SERVES 2	
PER SERVING:	
CALORIES	783
FAT	59G
PROTEIN	50G
SODIUM	1,476MG
FIBER	0G
CARBOHYDRATES	2G
NET CARBS	2G
SUGAR	1G

TIME	
PREP TIME:	5 MINUTES
COOK TIME:	20 MINUTES
TOTAL TIME:	25 MINUTES

TIPS & OPTIONS

Pair Go Go Grilled Cheese with a warm bowl of Minestrone Zippy Zoodle Soup (see Chapter 6) for the ultimate comfort food experience.

Bread substitute recipes can be calorie-dense. Be sure to add lots of vegetables to your meal to keep a healthy balance.

Want to take the ultimate shortcut? Reboot Boogie Bread (see Chapter 5) and slap on a slice of cheese. *Done.*

BARBECUE CHICKEN FLYING FLATBREAD

Enjoying homemade pizza on a regular basis has helped me to stay on track with DIRTY, LAZY, KETO. I don't feel resentful about missing out on favorite foods. In fact, I get fired up when challenged to create a low-carb alternative. My Barbecue Chicken Flying Flatbread recipe tastes just as good as what you'd experience at any restaurant— maybe even better, now that I think of it, as you can enjoy it at home in your slippers, *guilt-free*. You can't put a price on that!

Crust

1 cup superfine blanched almond flour

2 cups shredded whole milk mozzarella cheese

2 tablespoons full-fat cream cheese

1 large egg, beaten

¼ teaspoon salt

½ teaspoon baking powder

Toppings

¼ cup sugar-free barbecue sauce

2 Grab and Go Chicken Breasts, shredded (see Chapter 10)

½ cup shredded whole milk mozzarella cheese

1 medium clove garlic, peeled and minced

1 Preheat oven to 425°F. Line a baking sheet with parchment paper.

2 In a large microwave-safe bowl, combine almond flour, mozzarella, and cream cheese and microwave on high 1 minute. Stir and microwave another 30 seconds.

3 Mix in egg, salt, and baking powder until a dough forms.

4 Put dough on prepared baking sheet and flatten to no more than ¼" thickness in an oblong shape.

5 Bake 8–10 minutes until top begins to brown.

6 In a medium bowl, combine barbecue sauce and chicken. Mix well to coat.

7 Evenly spread barbecue chicken on crust. Top with mozzarella and garlic. Bake 5 minutes to melt cheese.

8 Cut into six even slices using a pizza cutter and serve warm.

NAAN NOW

NET CARBS

5G

SERVES 4

PER SERVING:

CALORIES	528
FAT	41G
PROTEIN	27G
SODIUM	720MG
FIBER	4G
CARBOHYDRATES	9G
NET CARBS	5G
SUGAR	2G

TIME

PREP TIME:	6 MINUTES
COOK TIME:	24 MINUTES
TOTAL TIME:	30 MINUTES

TIPS & OPTIONS »

If the dough is too dry, stir in a teaspoon of water until it's workable (but not sticky). Chill in fridge if needed to firm up and remove stickiness.

Get inspired by the variety of naan served in restaurants. Garlic, onion, and cilantro are popular styles of naan.

Tandoori breads like this are traditionally cooked on the walls of high-temperature clay ovens. The final appearance looks scarred, bubbled, and often charred, making it one of the most forgiving dishes to make!

Indian food and DLK are a match made in heaven. Many of the sauces (like my favorite Butter Chicken) are rich with healthy fat and protein (but low in carbohydrates). The conundrum about Indian food lies in the starchy side dishes—Indian buffets offer rice or naan bread with every meal. I sidestep these sides altogether and instead choose shredded lettuce or my homemade Naan Now bread. *Namaste.*

1½ tablespoons plain full-fat Greek yogurt

2½ cups shredded whole milk mozzarella cheese

2 medium eggs, beaten

2 teaspoons baking powder

1¼ cups superfine blanched almond flour

2 tablespoons unsalted butter, melted

1 medium clove garlic, peeled and minced

1 tablespoon finely chopped fresh cilantro

1 Preheat oven to 400°F. Line a baking sheet with parchment paper.

2 In a medium microwave-safe bowl, add yogurt and mozzarella and microwave on high 1 minute. Stir and microwave again 1 minute.

3 In a separate medium bowl, whisk eggs, baking powder, and almond flour together.

4 Stir egg mixture into cheese mixture until dough forms.

5 Cut dough into four equal pieces and form each into a ball. Press dough onto prepared baking sheet until they are in typical naan oval shape and ¼"–½" thick.

6 Bake 7–10 minutes until golden and firm.

7 In a small bowl, whisk butter, garlic, and cilantro until combined.

8 Remove naan from oven. Brush tops with garlic butter and bake again 12 minutes until starting to brown.

9 Serve warm.

TEMPO TORTILLAS

Walking away from tortillas can be excruciating for some. When a food like naan, rice, or tortillas is ingrained into your culture, removing it from the diet can seem sacrilegious. If a food represents more to you than just flavor, I recommend finding a new, healthier way to make the dish. You don't want a single food to cause any resentment, right? Tempo Tortillas quickly cut the carbs while maintaining the form and function of a tortilla.

4 large egg whites

1 tablespoon olive oil

3 tablespoons coconut flour

¼ teaspoon baking powder

⅛ teaspoon salt

⅛ teaspoon ground black pepper

1   In a medium mixing bowl, combine all ingredients and whisk to fully blend.

2   In a small nonstick skillet over medium heat, add half of the batter. Using a silicone spatula, carefully spread dough to edges of pan, creating a circular shape approximately 6" in diameter. Cook 3–4 minutes until tortilla bottom begins to brown. Use spatula to pry up edge and flip over, cooking 3–4 minutes more on opposite side. Remove.

3   Repeat to create second tortilla. Serve warm.

NET CARBS	
3G	

SERVES 2	
PER SERVING:	
CALORIES	138
FAT	8G
PROTEIN	9G
SODIUM	322MG
FIBER	4G
CARBOHYDRATES	7G
NET CARBS	3G
SUGAR	3G

TIME	
PREP TIME:	4 MINUTES
COOK TIME:	16 MINUTES
TOTAL TIME:	20 MINUTES

TIPS & OPTIONS

You also have the option of making larger tortillas (like for making a burrito). Use a bigger skillet and double or quadruple the recipe to make the desired shape.

Serve warm as a side dish or use as a soft taco and insert your favorite toppings.

These days, there are many low-carb tortilla options available at the grocery store (some tasting better than others!). La Tortilla Factory brand has never let me down.

READY OR NOT CORN BREAD

I've had an ongoing battle about corn with one of my family members. He happens to be from Nebraska, where corn is an economically important crop. Just because corn is a vegetable doesn't mean it's healthy (at least for me, anyway!). Corn is too starchy and high in carbs for my liking. I can survive without it. (Though I'm still a little sad about popcorn, I'll admit.) I made Ready or Not Corn Bread to prove my point.

1 cup superfine blanched almond flour

2 tablespoons coconut flour

½ tablespoon baking powder

½ teaspoon salt

2 tablespoons full-fat sour cream

¼ cup unsalted butter, melted

2 medium eggs, beaten

12 drops liquid 0g net carbs sweetener

½ cup shredded Cheddar cheese

3 tablespoons unsalted butter

¼ cup sugar-free pancake syrup

1 Preheat oven to 375°F. Grease a 9" × 7" baking dish.

2 In a medium mixing bowl, whisk together flours, baking powder, and salt.

3 In a separate medium mixing bowl, stir to combine sour cream, melted butter, eggs, and sweetener.

4 Stir dry mixture into wet mixture until thoroughly combined.

5 Fold in Cheddar until thoroughly mixed and then spread evenly in prepared baking dish.

6 Bake 25 minutes until firm and golden.

7 Slice and serve warm with remaining butter and sugar-free pancake syrup drizzled on top of each serving.

NET CARBS
2G

SERVES 9

PER SERVING:

CALORIES	214
FAT	18G
PROTEIN	6G
SODIUM	287MG
FIBER	2G
CARBOHYDRATES	5G
NET CARBS	2G
SUGAR	1G
SUGAR ALCOHOL	1G

TIME

PREP TIME:	5 MINUTES
COOK TIME:	25 MINUTES
TOTAL TIME:	30 MINUTES

TIPS & OPTIONS

Serve with barbecued chicken and grilled veggies for an A+ summertime experience.

Butter and syrup make everything taste better. No one will notice the lack of corn with a little bit of *deliciousness* on top!

ZUCCHINI ZOOM ZOOM BREAD

TIPS & OPTIONS

I love a little butter and jam on my zucchini bread. *Don't knock it till you try it!* I keep a bottle of Smucker's Sugar Free Strawberry Preserves in my refrigerator for moments like this. It has 2 grams net carbs per tablespoon. Other Smucker's sugar-free preserve flavors you might enjoy include red raspberry, blueberry, orange marmalade, and apricot.

One Christmas a couple of decades ago (am I THAT old?), I received a fancy-pants bread maker for my "big gift." Boy, did I put that gift to use! My kitchen smelled like a bakery for months. I had fallen victim to the marketing ploy that food from scratch was somehow "healthier." I even convinced myself that homemade *whole-wheat* bread would help me lose weight. Boy, was I wrong on both counts. Since DLK, I have had to become more open-minded about what constitutes bread in order to cut the carbs—lettuce leaves, low-carb tortillas, and Zucchini Zoom Zoom Bread are now among my favorites.

1½ cups shredded zucchini	3 tablespoons coconut flour
3 large eggs	½ teaspoon baking soda
¼ cup unsalted butter, softened	½ teaspoon baking powder
½ teaspoon pure vanilla extract	¼ teaspoon salt
¼ cup 0g net carbs sweetener	¼ teaspoon ground cinnamon
¾ cup superfine blanched almond flour	⅛ teaspoon ground nutmeg
	¼ cup chopped walnuts

1 Preheat oven to 350°F. Grease a twelve-cup muffin tin.

2 Using a cheesecloth, squeeze excess moisture from zucchini.

3 In a medium mixing bowl, whisk together eggs, butter, vanilla, and sweetener.

4 In a separate medium bowl, combine all dry ingredients except nuts. Combine wet and dry ingredients in one bowl and mix well. Lastly, fold in zucchini and nuts.

5 Scoop equal amounts of batter into prepared muffin cups. Bake 23–25 minutes until firm and a toothpick comes out dry when poked into the middle of one.

6 Serve warm.

CHAPTER 9

SIDES

Side dishes are important accessories to the main event. They're like a terrific pair of earrings, a necklace, or a matching bracelet that accentuates your ensemble. Sides can complement (or ruin!) the whole look of what you're pulling together. With a little planning, I'll help you design the perfect DIRTY, LAZY, KETO outfit.

High-carb sides dishes (like rolls, chips, or toast) are easy to dismiss. You can tell the waiter, "No rice or tortillas, please" and be done worrying about carbs, right? *Not so fast.* Sometimes your meal is much more complicated to plan. Higher-carb side dishes can be difficult to identify. They look seemingly "healthy" but are actually quite high in carbs. Take vegetables, for example. Often some of the most offensive side dishes contain higher-carb vegetables such as corn on the cob, peas, or sweet potatoes. Since these are touted as "good for you," they might slip under your DIRTY, LAZY, KETO radar. *You've been warned!*

But more often than not, higher-carb side dishes are easy to spot. In my previous "heavier life," every entrée was served with a heavy starch as its side dish. Rice, potatoes, pasta, or bread hogged at least half of my dinner plate! If the starch wasn't on the side, it was hiding underneath, like a plate of noodles under spaghetti sauce or a bed of rice with curry sauce poured on top. Most entrées, it seemed, were pre-programmed to have a starchy best friend. The two seemed inseparable. It was illogical to NOT eat these foods together!

Learning to redefine side dishes took time. At first, I wouldn't let go. I searched high and low for a lower-starch version of the same item. These exist but are usually hard to find in stores (and quite expensive). Like you, I tried the "fake" *fishy* noodles and low-carb *cardboard* bread. *So disappointing!* Eventually, I gave up looking for a miracle product. I learned to create my own DIRTY, LAZY, KETO low-carb version of side dishes or pair an old favorite with a new food altogether. This shift in mindset has increased my overall happiness level (and ability to "stick with it") a hundred times over. I encourage you to do the same.

GOBBLE GOBBLE GREEN BEAN CASSEROLE

Holidays don't have to be boring just because you're committed to DIRTY, LAZY, KETO. In fact, you can still enjoy many traditional favorites, like Gobble Gobble Green Bean Casserole! All it takes is a little creativity when it comes to the ingredients. Instead of the *carb-loaded* fried onion topping many of us grew up with, try sprinkling a tablespoon of crumbled bacon or crushed pork rinds on top after the bake. This dish is sure to replace Grandma's version without any complaints.

1 teaspoon olive oil

1 cup thinly sliced mushrooms

¼ cup chopped green onion

1 teaspoon minced garlic

1 pound fresh green beans, steamed, trimmed, and cut into 1" sections

½ tablespoon Italian seasoning

2 strips no-sugar-added bacon, cooked and crumbled

½ cup heavy whipping cream

½ tablespoon soy sauce

¼ cup shredded whole milk mozzarella cheese

⅛ teaspoon ground black pepper

1 teaspoon grated Parmesan cheese

1 Preheat oven to 375°F. Grease a 9" × 9" baking dish.

2 In a large skillet over medium heat, heat oil. Stir in mushrooms, onion, and garlic. Cook 4–5 minutes, stirring occasionally, until mixture starts to brown.

3 Add green beans and remaining ingredients, except Parmesan, and stir to combine.

4 Pour into prepared baking dish, cover with aluminum foil, and bake 10 minutes. Remove foil and return to oven to bake 5 minutes more to brown top.

5 Let cool slightly. Stir and serve warm with sprinkle of Parmesan on top.

NET CARBS
3G

SERVES 6	
PER SERVING:	
CALORIES	139
FAT	10G
PROTEIN	5G
SODIUM	183MG
FIBER	3G
CARBOHYDRATES	6G
NET CARBS	3G
SUGAR	3G

TIME	
PREP TIME:	10 MINUTES
COOK TIME:	20 MINUTES
TOTAL TIME:	30 MINUTES

TIPS & OPTIONS

Use canned mushrooms or canned green beans instead. Even frozen green beans can be substituted for fresh in this recipe, as long as they are cooked and ready to go!

This is a great dish for sneaking in vegetables. They kind of disappear in the thick and creamy sauce—all that people will see are the green beans. Broccoli, cauliflower, bell peppers, and even eggplant can be buried in this dish. Of course, if relatives are expecting the *traditional* green bean casserole, this strategy might cause an uproar.

ASAP ASPARAGUS WITH "HOLIDAY" SAUCE

Asparagus spears are the French fries of DIRTY, LAZY, KETO. *Seriously!* When cooked right, they can be just as crispy and delicious as fries from Micky D's. (Come on, folks, work with me a little.) Want to make asparagus irresistible? Add hollandaise sauce to the equation. Holla!

Asparagus

1½ pounds large asparagus spears, trimmed

¼ teaspoon salt

⅛ teaspoon ground black pepper

"Holiday" Sauce

2 large egg yolks

½ cup unsalted butter, melted

1 tablespoon 100% lemon juice

¼ teaspoon salt

⅛ teaspoon ground black pepper

1 Preheat oven to 400°F. Line a baking sheet with parchment paper.

2 In a large microwave-safe bowl, add asparagus and microwave on high 3–4 minutes until tender. Toss with salt and pepper and let cool.

3 In the bottom of a double boiler over medium-high heat, add 1" water. Heat until water begins to boil. Reduce heat to low.

4 In the top pan of the double boiler, whisk together egg yolks.

5 Very (very!) slowly, pour melted butter into sauce, continuing to whisk at a rapid pace until desired thickness is achieved. Add lemon juice, salt, and pepper and stir.

6 Remove from heat and set aside.

7 Spread out asparagus on prepared baking sheet and bake 10–12 minutes until starting to get crispy, turning halfway through.

8 Place asparagus on a serving platter and top with "Holiday" Sauce. Serve warm.

NET CARBS	
3G	

SERVES 6	
PER SERVING:	
CALORIES	176
FAT	16G
PROTEIN	4G
SODIUM	200MG
FIBER	2G
CARBOHYDRATES	5G
NET CARBS	3G
SUGAR	2G

TIME	
PREP TIME:	10 MINUTES
COOK TIME:	16 MINUTES
TOTAL TIME:	26 MINUTES

TIPS & OPTIONS

For a crispier asparagus, lightly coat each spear with cooking oil.

If you are a master of the broiler feature in your oven, try cooking the asparagus on high 5–6 minutes per side. You have to really babysit it, though! At least at my house, the broiler has a tendency to burn my food if I look away even for a second.

Save time and reboot Hollandaise Sauce from Early Eggs with Benefits (see Chapter 5).

GALLOPING GRITS

NET CARBS

3G

SERVES 4

PER SERVING:

CALORIES	148
FAT	6G
PROTEIN	17G
SODIUM	839MG
FIBER	2G
CARBOHYDRATES	5G
NET CARBS	3G
SUGAR	2G

TIME

PREP TIME:	5 MINUTES
COOK TIME:	25 MINUTES
TOTAL TIME:	30 MINUTES

When I'm out traveling, I make it a habit to stop by local grocery stores to pick up regional spices. They're inexpensive and easy to pack in my suitcase! On a recent trip to New Orleans, I bought a jar of "Slap Ya Mama" Cajun Seasoning. Call me sentimental, but sprinkling this spice on my Galloping Grits recipe makes the whole dish sing like a Dixieland band. Plus, when I run out of the souvenir spice, I have an excuse to go back.

1 (10-ounce) bag frozen riced cauliflower

2 tablespoons unsalted butter

1 pound medium (41–60 per pound) shrimp, peeled and deveined

1 tablespoon Cajun seasoning

1 teaspoon minced garlic

1   In a medium microwave-safe bowl, add riced cauliflower and microwave on high 4–5 minutes until tender.

2   In a large skillet over medium heat, melt butter. Stir in shrimp and seasoning and cook 10 minutes covered while stirring.

3   Add riced cauliflower and garlic. Stir to combine.

4   Cook covered 10 minutes, stirring regularly.

5   Serve warm.

TIPS & OPTIONS

Don't have any shrimp on hand? Don't trip! Substitute a different protein of your choice.

I recommend that you keep multiple bags of riced cauliflower in your freezer. They don't take up much room and are perfect for a multitude of recipes. To save time, I try to only buy the brands that can be microwaved directly in the bag.

HELP ME OUT HUSH PUPPIES

Don't get your knickers in a knot. You can still enjoy southern-style food and lose weight! Set up the table on the porch because I'm *a-fixin'* "K.F.C." Keto Fried Chicken (from *The DIRTY, LAZY, KETO® Cookbook*), Help Me Out Hush Puppies, and a pitcher of Snappy and Sweet Iced Tea (see Chapter 11) for supper tonight.

> 3 tablespoons full-fat cream cheese, softened
>
> 2 tablespoons unsalted butter, melted
>
> 2 large eggs, beaten
>
> 2½ tablespoons coconut flour
>
> 2 tablespoons grated yellow onion
>
> ½ teaspoon baking powder
>
> ½ teaspoon Creole seasoning
>
> ½ teaspoon minced garlic

1 Preheat oven to 375°F. Line a baking sheet with parchment paper.

2 In a large bowl, whisk together cream cheese, butter, and eggs.

3 Stir in remaining ingredients until completely mixed.

4 Form six even patties of dough no more than ½" thick. Carefully place on baking sheet ½" apart. Bake 20–25 minutes until golden and firm. Flip halfway through.

5 Serve warm.

NET CARBS

2G

SERVES 6

PER SERVING:

CALORIES	96
FAT	7G
PROTEIN	3G
SODIUM	209MG
FIBER	1G
CARBOHYDRATES	3G
NET CARBS	2G
SUGAR	1G

TIME

PREP TIME:	5 MINUTES
COOK TIME:	25 MINUTES
TOTAL TIME:	30 MINUTES

TIPS & OPTIONS

I use a cheese grater to grate small amounts of vegetables like the onion in this recipe (which saves so much time compared to hauling out my Cuisinart food processor and cleaning it afterward).

Prefer a firmer shape? Bake hush puppies inside well-greased cupcake tins.

Alternatively, you can fry your Help Me Out Hush Puppies. Any high-temperature oil will do: avocado, canola, corn, grape-seed, peanut, sunflower, and so on.

FASTEN YOUR SEATBELTS FONDUE

NET CARBS	
3G	

SERVES 8	
PER SERVING:	
CALORIES	159
FAT	10G
PROTEIN	8G
SODIUM	446MG
FIBER	1G
CARBOHYDRATES	4G
NET CARBS	3G
SUGAR	2G

TIME	
PREP TIME:	10 MINUTES
COOK TIME:	20 MINUTES
TOTAL TIME:	30 MINUTES

TIPS & OPTIONS

The spinach and artichoke hearts added to the cheese mixture can be fresh, frozen, or canned. They will meld with the cheeses so no one will be able to tell the difference.

Instead of a traditional fondue pot (what, you don't have one of these?), serve cheese dip in a mini Crock-Pot (with temperature on low).

Pre-make the fondue and bring to your next party! Serve with skewers of veggies and maybe even fresh bread for non-DLK folks.

To my family's horror, I once dragged them to a fondue-style restaurant. Everything protein on the menu came to the table raw with pots of boiling oil and long skewers used to cook it yourself. "It will be fun!" I insisted. My husband disagreed. "Why would anyone want to prepare their own food at a restaurant?" He may have been right. Touching raw chicken and steak while eating out? Kind of gross, actually. Today's Fasten Your Seatbelts Fondue recipe removes all the ick but keeps the novelty. Only veggies and cheese today, friends!

2 teaspoons minced garlic

1 cup dry sauvignon blanc wine

1 cup finely chopped spinach

¾ cup chopped artichoke hearts

1 cup shredded Cheddar cheese

1 cup shredded whole milk mozzarella cheese

6 tablespoons full-fat cream cheese, softened

1 teaspoon 100% lemon juice

¼ teaspoon salt

⅛ teaspoon ground black pepper

1 cup sliced zucchini rounds

1 cup bite-sized celery pieces

1 cup bite-sized broccoli florets

1   In a large nonstick skillet over medium heat, add garlic. Cook 2–3 minutes while stirring until soft.

2   Stir in wine, spinach, and artichokes and bring to boil. Reduce heat to low and simmer 5 minutes.

3   Slowly stir in cheeses, cream cheese, lemon juice, salt, and pepper. Keep stirring over low heat 12 minutes until smooth.

4   Put zucchini, celery, and broccoli in three separate small bowls.

5   Transfer cheese mixture to a fondue pot and serve while still smooth and warm with bowls of vegetables. Each person gets a skewer to use for dipping the vegetables.

BROCCOLI-BOOSTED CHEESE FRITTERS

My son helps me a lot in the kitchen. He hopes to open his own restaurant someday, and therefore, I hope to eat there for free (perks of knowing the boss). Despite his career aspirations, I consider my littlest Laska a picky eater. Sometimes it's a struggle to get him to eat heathy vegetables. Does that sound familiar? If so, I've got a solution: Broccoli-Boosted Cheese Fritters. They're like bite-sized healthy nuggets of *deliciousness*. As my teenager said (while popping the whole batch in his mouth before I could even eat one), "I could totally eat ALL of these!"

1 cup frozen riced broccoli

½ cup shredded whole milk mozzarella cheese

¼ cup superfine blanched almond flour

1 large egg, beaten

2 tablespoons finely chopped green onion

2 strips no-sugar-added bacon, cooked and finely crumbled

1 teaspoon minced garlic

½ teaspoon Creole seasoning

⅛ teaspoon salt

1. Preheat oven to 400°F. Line a baking sheet with parchment paper.

2. In a medium microwave-safe bowl, add broccoli and microwave on high 3–4 minutes until tender. Let cool and put in a colander to drain.

3. In a large bowl, add all ingredients and stir to combine.

4. Make 1" balls using a tablespoon and spread them out no less than 1" apart on prepared baking sheet.

5. Bake 20 minutes. Serve warm.

SHORT ORDER SRIRACHA BRUSSELS SPROUTS

I first fell in love with roasted Brussels sprouts when I ordered them from the BJ's Brewhouse appetizer menu. How did they get them so charred and delicious, yet so creamy? Up until then, I had only enjoyed them steamed (which is really boring in comparison). This five-gold-star recipe (awarded by myself, *to myself*) took several attempts on my part. I had to master the charring abilities of my broiler. I guarantee Short Order Sriracha Brussels Sprouts will become one of your all-time favorites too!

Brussels Sprouts

1 (12-ounce) bag Brussels sprouts

1 cup water

¼ cup olive oil

½ teaspoon salt

Sweet Sriracha Sauce

½ cup full-fat mayonnaise

1 teaspoon sriracha sauce

4 (1-gram) packets 0g net carbs sweetener

1. Preheat broiler to high. Line a baking sheet with foil. Grease foil with nonstick cooking spray.

2. Fit the metal trivet into an Instant Pot®. Add Brussels sprouts to steamer basket and place on trivet. Add water, put on lid, and close pressure release. Cook on High Pressure 5 minutes.

3. Carefully quick-release pressure and remove lid. Drain sprouts in a colander until cool enough to handle. Transfer sprouts to a medium bowl.

4. Add oil and salt. Toss to coat.

5. Spread sprouts out on prepared baking sheet. Broil 1–2 minutes until turning crispy. Turn and broil another 1–2 minutes until crispy on the other side.

6. In a small bowl, whisk all Sweet Sriracha Sauce ingredients until combined and sweetener is dissolved. Transfer to a small dipping bowl.

7. Serve warm Brussels sprouts on a large plate with bowl of Sweet Sriracha Sauce.

NET CARBS

5G

SERVES 4

PER SERVING:

CALORIES	344
FAT	33G
PROTEIN	3G
SODIUM	511MG
FIBER	3G
CARBOHYDRATES	8G
NET CARBS	5G
SUGAR	2G

TIME

PREP TIME:	5 MINUTES
COOK TIME:	9 MINUTES
TOTAL TIME:	14 MINUTES

TIPS & OPTIONS

If your sprouts come in microwave-safe packaging, then skip the Instant Pot® cooking steps and follow the cooking instructions on the bag.

Of course, the seasonings can be adjusted to your family's personal tastes (especially the amount of sriracha added for heat).

Smaller-sized Brussels sprouts (when halved) may not need to be "precooked" in the Instant Pot® as they will cook quickly and completely under the broiler.

Have an air fryer? Cook and crisp 15 minutes at 380°F.

ONION RUN RINGS

Comfort food cravings don't go away just because your eating habits become healthier. After all, we eat for reasons beyond hunger, right? I've had great success in my own weight loss journey by leaning in to these cravings as opposed to fighting them. By re-creating comfort food classics like onion rings with lower-carb ingredients, I'm able to stay on track with weight loss and maintenance without skipping a beat.

2 large yellow onions, peeled and sliced into ½" rings

1¼ cups superfine blanched almond flour

½ tablespoon baking powder

½ tablespoon Creole seasoning

½ cup half and half

½ cup water

1 large egg, beaten

1½ cups finely crushed pork rinds

2 cups vegetable oil

1 Separate all onion slices into rings and save acceptable rings of at least 1" diameter.

2 In a medium mixing bowl, combine almond flour, baking powder, and seasoning.

3 In a large Ziploc bag, add onion rings and 1½ tablespoons dry mixture. Seal and shake bag until all rings are coated.

4 Add half and half, water, and egg to remaining dry mixture and whisk until mixed thoroughly. Spread pork rinds on a large dinner plate.

5 In a medium skillet over medium heat, preheat oil to 375°F. Line a large plate with paper towels.

6 Dip each onion ring completely in batter and shake off excess. Transfer to plate with pork rinds and coat completely.

7 Gently drop coated rings in hot oil and deep-fry 2 minutes each until golden. Deep-fry 4–6 at time, approximately 20 minutes total. Transfer to lined plate to drain and cool.

8 Serve warm.

NET CARBS

4G

SERVES 8

PER SERVING:

CALORIES	256
FAT	20G
PROTEIN	10G
SODIUM	363MG
FIBER	2G
CARBOHYDRATES	6G
NET CARBS	4G
SUGAR	3G

TIME

PREP TIME:	10 MINUTES
COOK TIME:	20 MINUTES
TOTAL TIME:	30 MINUTES

TIPS & OPTIONS

Don't skip the Ziploc bag step for coating the onion rings. It's necessary to remove moisture from the exposed surfaces of the onion and will help the batter to stick.

Use tongs to dip rings in batter. Set down coated rings on the plate of crushed pork rinds, then spoon rinds over the top to fully coat. Shake off loose rinds that aren't attached.

Dip your cooked rings in rebooted homemade DLK House Ranch Dressing (see recipe for Hurry Up House Salad with Ranch in Chapter 6) or rebooted Wasabi Ranch Dip (see recipe for Drive-Thru Nuggets with Wasabi Ranch Dip in Chapter 10).

BRISK BROCCOLI ALFREDO

NET CARBS

9G

SERVES 4

PER SERVING:

CALORIES	323
FAT	28G
PROTEIN	6G
SODIUM	310MG
FIBER	2G
CARBOHYDRATES	11G
NET CARBS	9G
SUGAR	3G

TIME

PREP TIME:	10 MINUTES
COOK TIME:	14 MINUTES
TOTAL TIME:	24 MINUTES

TIPS & OPTIONS ≫

For a more robust meal, top with your favorite protein (grilled shrimp, chicken, and so on).

Just like at Olive Garden, everything tastes better with grated Parmesan cheese sprinkled on top. Go for it!

Freeze leftover portions of your homemade Alfredo sauce to enjoy another time. If properly sealed, it will last weeks in the freezer.

I learned about the Brisk Broccoli Alfredo combination on a recent trip to Olive Garden. My family was digging into plates of all-you-can-eat pasta while I sat disappointed with my unlimited bowl of salad (definitely not the same thing). Then it hit me… Alfredo sauce! Adding Alfredo sauce to, well, anything really tastes like heaven. It's impossible to feel deprived when enjoying Alfredo sauce on broccoli, salmon, *or even your spoon*.

1 (12-ounce) bag broccoli florets
2 tablespoons unsalted butter
1 cup heavy whipping cream
¼ cup grated Parmesan cheese
¼ teaspoon minced garlic
¼ teaspoon salt
⅛ teaspoon ground black pepper

1 In a medium microwave-safe bowl, add broccoli and microwave on high 3–4 minutes until softened but not mushy.

2 In a large skillet over medium heat, melt butter. Add broccoli and cook 5 minutes while stirring to lightly brown.

3 Stir in remaining ingredients and cook an additional 5 minutes.

4 Serve warm on four plates.

STRAIGHTAWAY SHEET PAN VEGETABLE MEDLEY

If you find yourself saying "I hate vegetables," this might be the recipe for you to try first. Even the pickiest eaters cave after tasting *roasted* vegetables. There is something magical about cooking them at high temperatures. Many vegetable flavors become sweeter (surprising, right?). Now that I've piqued your curiosity, let's get cookin' with Straightaway Sheet Pan Vegetable Medley.

¼ cup sesame oil

2 tablespoons balsamic vinegar

1 tablespoon chopped fresh basil

1 medium clove garlic, peeled and minced

½ teaspoon ground ginger

¼ teaspoon salt

¼ teaspoon ground black pepper

2½ cups bite-sized broccoli florets

1½ cups bite-sized cauliflower florets

1 medium green bell pepper, seeded and chopped

½ large red onion, peeled and sliced in rings

1 cup chopped zucchini

1 Preheat oven to 400°F. Line a baking sheet with parchment paper.

2 In a large bowl, whisk together oil, vinegar, basil, garlic, ginger, salt, and black pepper. Add all vegetables to bowl and stir until completely coated.

3 Transfer vegetables to baking sheet. Space them out so vegetables can cook on all sides.

4 Bake 15–20 minutes, turning regularly, until vegetables start to brown. Cover with foil if they start to brown before they are tender.

5 Serve warm.

NET CARBS
6G

SERVES 6

PER SERVING:

CALORIES	118
FAT	9G
PROTEIN	2G
SODIUM	121MG
FIBER	2G
CARBOHYDRATES	8G
NET CARBS	6G
SUGAR	3G

TIME

PREP TIME:	10 MINUTES
COOK TIME:	20 MINUTES
TOTAL TIME:	30 MINUTES

TIPS & OPTIONS

Use whatever vegetables you have on hand. Be creative! The sheet pan strategy is perfect for using up assorted leftover fresh veggies.

Try different spices or dipping sauces to make eating vegetables more fun (or tolerable, depending on your perspective).

Cut the vegetables into small bite-sized pieces (or smaller) to ensure that they cook completely.

STOPWATCH SPANISH "RICE"

NET CARBS

4G

SERVES 4

PER SERVING:
CALORIES	85
FAT	5G
PROTEIN	2G
SODIUM	267MG
FIBER	3G
CARBOHYDRATES	7G
NET CARBS	4G
SUGAR	3G

TIME

PREP TIME:	10 MINUTES
COOK TIME:	20 MINUTES
TOTAL TIME:	30 MINUTES

TIPS & OPTIONS

Cook a little longer uncovered to boil off the liquid if the dish is still too "soupy." The finished product should be crumbly and resemble a dry rice dish.

Buy small portions of frozen riced cauliflower in "direct to microwave" packaging to save time.

Frozen riced cauliflower (purchased in bulk bags) can be poured directly into a frying pan. (There is no need to defrost ahead of time.)

Prefer fresh? Make your own riced cauliflower by running heads of cauliflower through your food processor. Scrape with a rubber spatula often, and gently pulse machine for best results.

Cauliflower is the most miraculous of all DIRTY, LAZY, KETO ingredients. It takes on the flavor of whatever surrounds it, and it can be cooked in at least a dozen ways. It's affordable and available year-round, too, which removes all excuses. Even so, I find myself stocking up on frozen riced cauliflower whenever I catch a good sale. Having the right ingredients on hand makes it that much easier to cook a quick dish like Stopwatch Spanish "Rice."

> 2 tablespoons unsalted butter
> 1 (10-ounce) bag frozen riced cauliflower
> ½ medium green bell pepper, seeded and finely chopped
> ¼ cup chopped green onion
> ½ cup no-sugar-added diced tomatoes with green chiles, drained
> 1 tablespoon taco seasoning

1   In a large skillet over medium heat, melt butter. Stir in cauliflower and cook 10 minutes while stirring.

2   Stir in remaining ingredients and cook an additional 10 minutes while stirring to remove excess moisture.

3   Serve warm.

CHAPTER 10

MAIN DISHES

I have a confession to make. Last year at Thanksgiving, I didn't *aaaaaactually* make the turkey! (Sorry, Mom.) This might not be a big deal for most folks, but *helllloooo!* I'm a cookbook writer! *That's really embarrassing.* It's not that I didn't know how to bake the bird; I just chose not to. At the time, I felt overwhelmed with work. I was up against a deadline and running out of time. I needed to cut a few corners with meal planning to keep afloat. I made my favorite side dishes, but the main event? I called an outsider for help. *Gobble, gobble!*

In today's world, where all of us are pressed for time, we need to embrace more shortcuts in the kitchen to stay sane. Whether or not you own up to these tricks *in front of guests* is entirely up to you! (Maybe your mother-in-law doesn't need to know ALL of your secrets.) Either way, let's cut a few corners and stop wasting our valuable time. *Wash and chop romaine?* Buy a bag of prewashed lettuce instead. *Forget to thaw meat for dinner?* Toss the meat, solid as a rock, into the pressure cooker.

> You don't have to be perfect in the kitchen to be successful at weight loss.

Part of the reason I've been able to maintain my 140-pound weight loss for eight years is that I focus on the big picture: *eating healthy.* The details behind how this is executed are up for discussion. I don't stress over buying 100 percent fresh or only organic ingredients. The fish I grill probably isn't line-caught (unless reeling it from the bottom of my freezer counts?). Not every part of my meal is homemade either. No, this pesto isn't from scratch—*it's from Costco!* I don't rice my own cauliflower; no, ma'am. It's cheaper *and* faster to buy it frozen. I buy what's on sale. I cook with fresh, frozen, *and* canned ingredients. I am open-minded and realistic about taking cooking shortcuts.

There is no judgment with DIRTY, LAZY, KETO. Getting dinner ready is important, yes, but you've got to do it on your own terms.

READY, SET, GO GROUND BEEF

When I first met my husband, his fridge was full of jumbo cottage cheese containers. I was like, "What's with this guy? Nobody likes cottage cheese this much!" To my surprise, these containers were full of ingredients like cooked ground beef he was planning to use in his recipes. We were a match made in heaven. He taught me how to cook ahead (and be more budget-minded), and in exchange, I upgraded his bachelor ways to a more sophisticated food storage system—clear containers, to start with. It's much easier to utilize leftovers when you can actually see what's inside.

1 pound 93% lean ground beef

⅛ teaspoon salt

⅛ teaspoon ground black pepper

1   In a medium nonstick skillet over medium heat, cook beef 10 minutes while stirring.

2   Stir in salt and pepper and continue to cook 5 more minutes.

3   Let cool and refrigerate in an airtight container up to 4 days until ready to add to a meal.

NET CARBS

0G

SERVES 4

PER SERVING:	
CALORIES	166
FAT	7G
PROTEIN	24G
SODIUM	143MG
FIBER	0G
CARBOHYDRATES	0G
NET CARBS	0G
SUGAR	0G

TIME

PREP TIME:	5 MINUTES
COOK TIME:	15 MINUTES
TOTAL TIME:	20 MINUTES

TIPS & OPTIONS

Freeze unused portions to reboot for later meals. Use leftovers safely by thawing frozen meat (for reuse) in the refrigerator. When it's time for reheating, be sure the internal temperature reaches a minimum of 165°F or higher.

When storing leftovers safely in the refrigerator, airtight storage is key. Sealed Ziploc bags, secure plastic wrap, or plastic containers with properly fitting lids prevent bacteria from growing and keep your food safe.

This recipe (and storage tips) applies to all types of ground meat: turkey, chicken, pork, and so on.

GRAB AND GO CHICKEN BREASTS

TIPS & OPTIONS

Prefer the pressure cooker method? For the laziest chefs (like me!), cook boneless chicken breasts in an Instant Pot® on high pressure 8 minutes per pound.

Freeze unused portions to reboot for later meals. Use leftovers safely by thawing frozen meat (for reuse) in the refrigerator. When it's time for reheating, be sure the internal temperature reaches a minimum of 165°F or higher.

Ultra-lazy cooks can skip this recipe altogether and buy a precooked rotisserie chicken from the grocery store. Some stores even sell the meat already pulled from the bone in tidy packages. Now THAT'S convenient!

Cooking chicken ahead of time is just common sense. I use this ingredient in so many recipes, I'd be a fool to cook it over and over again throughout the week. *That's just too many dishes, people.* My time is valuable. If I can knock out a task in one sitting, sign me up! Plus, I find it convenient and cost-effective to cook chicken in bulk when I catch a good sale. The cooked leftovers are also easy to freeze for future meals.

4 (4.2-ounce) boneless, skinless chicken breasts

⅛ teaspoon salt

⅛ teaspoon ground black pepper

1 Preheat oven to 375°F. Grease a 9" × 12" × 2" baking dish.

2 Season breasts with salt and pepper and cook covered 25 minutes, flipping halfway through.

3 Let cool and refrigerate up to 4 days in an airtight container until ready to add to a meal.

BAM! BACON BURGERS

Is there any dish more American than a cheeseburger? I didn't think so! BAM! Bacon Burgers will be a hit with everyone in your household. If your family has been hesitant to support your new lifestyle change, make them this dish. After just one bite, you'll recruit a full team of volunteers to help "test" your recipes. Be sure to reboot leftover Onion Run Rings (see Chapter 9) and homemade DLK House Ranch Dressing here (see recipe for Hurry Up House Salad with Ranch in Chapter 6) for a complete DLK dining experience.

1 pound 93% lean ground beef

¼ cup grated yellow onion

2 tablespoons half and half

1 large egg, beaten

1 medium clove garlic, peeled and minced

½ teaspoon salt

¼ teaspoon ground black pepper

4 ounces sharp Cheddar cheese, cut into ¼"–½" cubes

½ pound thin-sliced no-sugar-added bacon, cut in half to make 3"–4" sections

1 Preheat oven to 400°F. Line a baking sheet with parchment paper.

2 In a medium bowl, thoroughly combine beef, onion, half and half, egg, garlic, salt, and pepper.

3 Use a scoop to form 1" balls. Push your index finger into the center of each ball and hide cube of cheese there. Pinch sides of hole you created to close and form back into ball with cheese cube sealed inside.

4 Wrap each ball in two half strips of bacon. Alternate directions, one right to left and second up and down, to ensure full coverage around ball.

5 Place on prepared baking sheet spaced at least ½" apart and bake 25 minutes, turning and draining fat regularly until meat is cooked throughout and bacon is crispy.

6 Serve warm.

NET CARBS
2G

SERVES 6	
PER SERVING:	
CALORIES	278
FAT	16G
PROTEIN	27G
SODIUM	630MG
FIBER	0G
CARBOHYDRATES	2G
NET CARBS	2G
SUGAR	1G

TIME	
PREP TIME:	5 MINUTES
COOK TIME:	25 MINUTES
TOTAL TIME:	30 MINUTES

TIPS & OPTIONS

I prefer the thin-sliced bacon as it forms better around the balls and also will be easier to bite through.

Use a simple box grater to shred the onion. Don't create a ton more work for yourself by dragging out your humongous food processor from storage and turning your house upside down searching for the right shredder attachment.

RUSH IN REUBEN

After finishing the New York City Marathon, I craved three things: a shower, an ice-cold Diet Coke, and a hot Reuben sandwich. I'd had 26.2 miles to think about what I wanted; nothing was going to get in my way (well, except the 52,812 other runners). I may not be in New York City anymore, but my Rush In Reuben recipe takes me back to the glory I felt after finishing the race. Rush In Reuben is the sandwich of champions.

Chaffle Buns
- ¼ cup superfine blanched almond flour
- ¼ cup full-fat cream cheese, softened
- ½ teaspoon baking powder
- ½ teaspoon garlic salt
- 2 large eggs, beaten
- 1 tablespoon unsalted butter, melted

Sandwich Toppings
- ½ pound sliced corned beef
- ½ pound sauerkraut, drained
- 2 (1-ounce) slices Swiss cheese
- 1 tablespoon Thousand Island dressing
- 2 tablespoons full-fat mayonnaise

1. Grease a mini waffle maker with nonstick spray and preheat.
2. In a medium bowl, whisk together Chaffle Buns ingredients and pour one-fourth of batter in center of hot waffle maker and close. Cook 3 minutes and remove bun to plate. Repeat for three more buns.
3. In a medium microwave-safe bowl, add corned beef and microwave on high 1½ minutes.
4. In a separate medium microwave-safe bowl, add sauerkraut and microwave on high 1½ minutes.
5. Place 1 bun on each of two plates. Top each with half of meat first, then half of sauerkraut, and finally, a slice of Swiss.
6. In a small bowl, stir to combine dressing and mayonnaise.
7. Spread each of remaining buns with half of dressing mixture. Place each bun, dressing side down, on each sandwich. Serve warm.

NET CARBS

7G

SERVES 2

PER SERVING:

CALORIES	848
FAT	65G
PROTEIN	40G
SODIUM	2,815MG
FIBER	5G
CARBOHYDRATES	12G
NET CARBS	7G
SUGAR	5G

TIME

PREP TIME:	10 MINUTES
COOK TIME:	15 MINUTES
TOTAL TIME:	25 MINUTES

TIPS & OPTIONS

Skip making the Chaffle Bun steps by rebooting Boogie Bread (see Chapter 5).

Be sure to purchase fresh sauerkraut (sold in the deli section of your grocery store) to enjoy the natural probiotic benefits from fermentation. Probiotics help maintain strong intestinal health. Emerging research suggests that balanced bacteria in the gut reduces overall inflammation and can prevent or treat a variety of illnesses. *Huh!*

Thousand Island dressing is higher in carbs compared to my usual DLK favorites (ranch or blue cheese dressing). This is why I "water it down" with mayonnaise.

EZ ZOODLE NOODLE "SPAGHETTI"

TIPS & OPTIONS

I've never had any luck with commercial spiralizers. If you like them, great. Otherwise, stick with a julienne peeler like me. This inexpensive handheld tool is much cheaper and doesn't take up any counter space.

Reboot leftover zoodles with the Minestrone Zippy Zoodle Soup recipe (see Chapter 6).

Instead of boiling your zoodles for 1 minute, try the stir-fry method instead. Heat a tablespoon of oil in a skillet over medium heat and gently toss zoodles until they reach desired softness.

I've tried many brands of shirataki noodles with little success. No matter how much rinsing I do, a fishy smell persists. This works well in seafood or broth recipes like pho, but definitely not with Italian-style spaghetti! Instead, I prefer making noodles from zucchini. This bland vegetable doesn't compete with flavors from added sauces. As an added bonus, zucchini is inexpensive, readily available, and quick to manipulate. For a recipe like EZ Zoodle Noodle "Spaghetti," zucchini is the best overall choice.

3 cups water

4 medium zucchini, ends trimmed

½ cup pesto

½ cup no-sugar-added pasta sauce

4 teaspoons grated Parmesan cheese

1 In a medium saucepan over medium heat, boil water.

2 To make zoodles by hand, use a julienne vegetable peeler and apply light pressure lengthwise down the entire (unpeeled) zucchini. Continue making long, thin strips until you work your way through the entire vegetable. Carefully add to boiling water for *1 minute only* to prevent them from getting too soft. Drain and divide evenly among four plates.

3 In a medium microwave-safe bowl, whisk pesto and pasta sauce together. Microwave on high 30 seconds. Stir and microwave again 30 seconds.

4 Top each mound of zoodles evenly with sauce. Sprinkle Parmesan on top.

5 Serve warm.

QUICK COVER UP COTTAGE PIE

A cottage pie is usually made with beef, while a shepherd's pie contains lamb. Either way, you're covering up a meat pie, people. What makes the DLK version special is how I change up the mashed potato "frosting." Mashed cauliflower, combined with rich cream and cheese, is a superior substitute, making this classic dish a homespun home run. As an added bonus, the "frosting" covers up the mystery meat, allowing you to sneak in leftovers from last night's dinner.

1½ (12-ounce) bags cauliflower florets, thawed

½ pound lean ground turkey

½ cup diced tomatoes

¼ cup chopped celery

⅓ cup chopped green onions

1 teaspoon minced garlic

½ cup heavy whipping cream

¼ cup shredded whole milk mozzarella cheese, softened

1 teaspoon Italian seasoning

¼ teaspoon salt

⅛ teaspoon ground black pepper

1 Preheat oven to 400°F. Grease a 9" × 7" × 2" baking dish.

2 In a large microwave-safe bowl, add cauliflower and microwave on high 5 minutes. Let cool.

3 While cauliflower is microwaving, in a medium nonstick skillet over medium heat, add turkey, tomatoes, celery, green onions, and garlic. Cook 10 minutes while stirring until soft and browning.

4 In a food processor, add cauliflower, cream, mozzarella, Italian seasoning, salt, and pepper. Pulse two to four times until desired "mashed potato" consistency is reached.

5 Spread even layer of meat mixture in baking dish. Top with even layer of cauliflower mixture.

6 Bake 10 minutes. Serve warm.

NET CARBS

5G

SERVES 4

PER SERVING:

CALORIES	255
FAT	17G
PROTEIN	17G
SODIUM	277MG
FIBER	4G
CARBOHYDRATES	9G
NET CARBS	5G
SUGAR	5G

TIME

PREP TIME:	10 MINUTES
COOK TIME:	20 MINUTES
TOTAL TIME:	30 MINUTES

TIPS & OPTIONS

Any ground protein, even tofu, can be substituted or even added to this dish. Also, get creative with the vegetables used. No one is going to say, "You can't do that!"

Baby eggplant, chayote, or jicama? These are all unusual vegetables that are right at home in a baked dish like this.

Quick Cover Up Cottage Pie may look shallow in a 9" × 7" baking dish, but using this size allows the dish to cook faster.

PRESTO CHICKEN PARMESAN

I avoided eating Italian food for the longest time. I was under the mistaken belief that plates of pasta had to accompany every meal—*or else*! I had to get over myself. The Italians have so much more to offer. I've learned to try the new Italian flavors of capers, anchovies, fresh herbs, and olives. Nevertheless, sometimes I crave a traditional favorite like Presto Chicken Parmesan.

¾ cup full-fat mayonnaise

¾ cup grated Parmesan cheese

1 medium clove garlic, peeled and minced

½ teaspoon salt

¼ teaspoon ground black pepper

4 (4.2-ounce) boneless, skinless chicken breasts

2 tablespoons unsalted butter

1 cup no-sugar-added pasta sauce

1 cup shredded whole milk mozzarella cheese

1   In a medium bowl, combine mayonnaise, Parmesan, garlic, salt, and pepper. Whisk until blended.

2   Place a large piece of parchment paper on your counter. Place chicken breasts on top and pound chicken to no thicker than ¾".

3   Pat dry and dredge breasts in mayonnaise mixture, being sure to coat both sides. Shake off extra.

4   In a large skillet over medium heat, melt butter. Fry all four breasts together for 10 minutes until golden. Flip and fry another 10 minutes.

5   In a medium microwave-safe bowl, add pasta sauce and microwave on high covered 30 seconds. Stir and microwave again for 30 seconds.

6   Remove each breast to a dinner plate. Spoon pasta sauce over chicken and top with equal amounts of mozzarella. Serve warm.

TIME PRESSURE COOKER BEEF STEW

NET CARBS

2G

SERVES 6

PER SERVING:
CALORIES	196
FAT	6G
PROTEIN	27G
SODIUM	628MG
FIBER	2G
CARBOHYDRATES	4G
NET CARBS	2G
SUGAR	2G

TIME

PREP TIME:	10 MINUTES
COOK TIME:	20 MINUTES
TOTAL TIME:	30 MINUTES

TIPS & OPTIONS ≫

Time Pressure Cooker Beef Stew often tastes better the next day after all of the flavors bloom and the stew thickens.

Enjoy your stew with a side of Ready or Not Corn Bread (see Chapter 8) and Hurry Up House Salad with Ranch (see Chapter 6).

There is nothing inherently wrong with comfort food. I bristle when experts suggest otherwise. Having emotional connections to food is normal! A delicious smell alone can take me back to childhood or remind me of a happy place in time. As long as I'm not baking cookies for comfort, I don't see anything wrong with nostalgia. Time Pressure Cooker Beef Stew is one of those recipes that warms the heart and fills your kitchen with memories.

1½ pounds rump roast, trimmed of fat and cubed into ¾" pieces

½ cup chopped celery

1 small carrot, peeled and thinly sliced

½ large yellow onion, peeled and chopped

2 tablespoons no-sugar-added tomato paste

1 cup beef broth

1 teaspoon salt

½ teaspoon ground black pepper

1 teaspoon xanthan gum

1 In a large bowl, add all ingredients except xanthan gum. Stir to combine and coat meat.

2 Put mixture in the Instant Pot®.

3 Put on lid and close pressure release. Cook on High Pressure 20 minutes. Carefully quick-release pressure and remove lid.

4 Sprinkle xanthan gum slowly into mixture while stirring to combine. Serve warm in soup bowls.

CHOP SUEY EXPRESS

"Get off the couch and see the world!" is one of my *Stephanie-isms*, or guiding life principles. I have so much energy after losing 140 pounds that on weekends, instead of watching TV, I drag my family on adventurous day trips. San Francisco's Chinatown tops the list as a family favorite. Walking up and down the hills gives us a good workout while we visit local shops, enjoy cultural parades, and of course, sit down to lunch. The menu is printed in Chinese, but I can still find my favorite Chop Suey (which, surprisingly, means "leftovers"!).

½ cup water

2 tablespoons unsalted butter, melted

½ cup chopped green bell pepper

½ cup sliced mushrooms

¼ cup chopped green onion

¼ cup chopped celery

½ cup snow peas, trimmed and cut in 1" sections

2 teaspoons minced garlic

¼ teaspoon ground black pepper

¾ cup soy sauce

½ tablespoon grated fresh ginger

¼ teaspoon ground cinnamon

2 pounds chuck roast beef, trimmed and diced into cubes no larger than ¾"

1   In a large bowl, add all ingredients. Stir to mix and coat meat.

2   Put mixture in the Instant Pot®.

3   Put on lid and close pressure release. Cook on High Pressure 20 minutes. Carefully quick-release pressure and remove lid.

4   Remove the trivet and give the pot a final stir. Serve warm.

NET CARBS

4G

SERVES 6

PER SERVING:

CALORIES	274
FAT	10G
PROTEIN	37G
SODIUM	1,841MG
FIBER	1G
CARBOHYDRATES	5G
NET CARBS	4G
SUGAR	1G

TIME

PREP TIME:	10 MINUTES
COOK TIME:	20 MINUTES
TOTAL TIME:	30 MINUTES

TIPS & OPTIONS

This is best served on a bed of cooked riced cauliflower.

Make sure that you serve with the very tasty gravy that is in the bottom of the pot. Slowly stir in ¼ teaspoon xanthan gum at a time to thicken if desired.

TURKEY TROT DRUMSTICKS

Though admittedly morbid, I find myself thoroughly entertained by stories of Thanksgiving turkeys gone wrong. Still-frozen turkeys, non-injury deep-fryer explosions, or dropped birds? I just can't help myself; I have to know more! Hearing horror stories like these immediately makes me feel like I'm doing a good job preparing the big meal. It can be stressful, right? Sometimes a laugh is just what we need to put it all in perspective. My Turkey Trot Drumsticks recipe will have your holiday meal on the table safe, sound, and stress-free.

6 cups peanut oil

1 tablespoon Creole seasoning

2 medium turkey legs (drumsticks)

2 ounces injectable Creole butter marinade

1   In a large soup pot over medium heat, preheat oil to 375°F. Line a plate with paper towels.

2   Rub Creole seasoning all over turkey legs.

3   Inject 1 ounce butter marinade into each leg (using included syringe) in several places under skin.

4   Carefully lower both legs into oil and deep-fry 15–20 minutes until internal temperature of the turkey legs reaches at least 165°F.

5   Remove legs from oil and place onto lined plate to drain and cool.

6   Serve warm.

NET CARBS

0G

SERVES 2

PER SERVING:

CALORIES	682
FAT	46G
PROTEIN	55G
SODIUM	2,914MG
FIBER	0G
CARBOHYDRATES	0G
NET CARBS	0G
SUGAR	0G

TIME

PREP TIME:	5 MINUTES
COOK TIME:	20 MINUTES
TOTAL TIME:	25 MINUTES

TIPS & OPTIONS

Double or triple this recipe to make good use of the prepared frying oil.

Don't worry if you don't have a plastic syringe to inject the butter marinade. Do your best to push the hard butter under the skin. Stand the leg on a plate with the fat end up. Pull the skin as loose as you can and push the butter down. Some will drain out when you lay the leg back down, so add sparingly. If you can, seal the butter marinade inside with toothpicks or food-grade string, and then *play on, playah!*

SNAPPY STUFFED SALMON

NET CARBS

2G

SERVES 4

PER SERVING:
CALORIES	442
FAT	27G
PROTEIN	40G
SODIUM	506MG
FIBER	0G
CARBOHYDRATES	2G
NET CARBS	2G
SUGAR	1G

TIME

PREP TIME:	15 MINUTES
COOK TIME:	12 MINUTES
TOTAL TIME:	27 MINUTES

TIPS & OPTIONS

No air fryer? No problem. Place salmon in a well-greased baking dish, cover with aluminum foil, and bake at 350°F about 30 minutes until fillets are flaky throughout.

Be sure to take out the trash tonight. No one wants to wake up to fish smell the next day.

Want another trick to save prep time in the kitchen? Instead of making the Salmon Stuffing from scratch, substitute fresh spinach-artichoke dip purchased from the deli. *Shhh!*

The first time I had this dish, I was dining at the top of the Space Needle in Seattle. I'm slightly afraid of heights, but I forgot all about my fears when a gorgeous plate of spinach-stuffed salmon arrived at the table. *Hello, beautiful!* I spent the rest of the evening trying to figure out how I could make it myself when I got home from my trip without spending all day in the kitchen. When choosing your fillets for this dish, make sure they are thick enough to slice horizontally and allow for stuffing.

Salmon Stuffing

½ cup chopped spinach

6 tablespoons full-fat cream cheese, softened

¾ cup shredded whole milk mozzarella cheese

2 teaspoons minced garlic

¼ teaspoon salt

⅛ teaspoon ground black pepper

Salmon Glaze

2 tablespoons olive oil

1½ tablespoons 100% lemon juice

⅛ teaspoon salt

⅛ teaspoon ground black pepper

Salmon Fillets

4 (6-ounce) salmon fillets

1 Grease bottom rack of air fryer drawer, then preheat air fryer to 400°F.

2 In a medium bowl, combine all Salmon Stuffing ingredients. Stir until well mixed.

3 In a small bowl, whisk to combine all Salmon Glaze ingredients.

4 Brush both sides of all 4 salmon fillets with Salmon Glaze.

5 Using a sharp knife, carefully slice each salmon fillet horizontally to create a deep pocket for stuffing.

6 Using a silicone spatula, slide equal amounts of Salmon Stuffing into each fillet.

7 Place fish on greased bottom rack in air fryer basket with plenty of space around each fillet.

8 Cook 10–12 minutes until fillets are flaky throughout. Serve warm.

HURRIED JALAPEÑO HOLLA CASSEROLE

Holla that a jalapeño casserole is on the table and prepare for a stampede at your house. My husband gets so excited about spicy food, he even loves jalapeño jelly. (Spicy jam? That's just wrong, people!) I, on the other hand, learned to love exotic food later in life. Once the burn of excessive Jolly Rancher eating wore off, my new and improved low-carb tongue was ready to take on new flavors. Unbeknownst to me, dishes like Hurried Jalapeño Holla Casserole would become my new normal. It's fast and easy to make, which makes me want to *holla* for more!

1 large cooked rotisserie chicken

¾ cup full-fat cream cheese, softened

1 cup half and half

3 tablespoons chicken broth

1 medium clove garlic, peeled and minced

¼ teaspoon salt

⅛ teaspoon ground black pepper

1 cup shredded Mexican-style cheese blend

1 cup sliced (in rings) jalapeño peppers

6 slices no-sugar-added bacon, cooked and crumbled

1 Preheat oven to 400°F. Grease a 9" × 9" baking dish.

2 Remove all meat from chicken and shred. Be sure not to include any skin or bones.

3 In a medium bowl, whisk cream cheese, half and half, broth, garlic, salt, and pepper.

4 Spread shredded chicken evenly in baking dish. Spread cream cheese mixture evenly over chicken.

5 Sprinkle cheese on top followed by jalapeños and bacon.

6 Bake 15–20 minutes until browning on top.

7 Serve warm.

DRIVE-THRU NUGGETS WITH WASABI RANCH DIP

When I find something delicious that works for me (easy to make, affordable, and within my net carb count), I tend to put that meal on repeat. Will Drive-Thru Nuggets with Wasabi Ranch Dip become your repeat offender?

NET CARBS
6G

SERVES 4

PER SERVING:	
CALORIES	610
FAT	47G
PROTEIN	30G
SODIUM	604MG
FIBER	2G
CARBOHYDRATES	8G
NET CARBS	6G
SUGAR	2G

TIME	
PREP TIME:	10 MINUTES
COOK TIME:	12 MINUTES
TOTAL TIME:	22 MINUTES

Chicken Nuggets
1 cup vegetable oil

¾ cup full-fat mayonnaise

3 teaspoons apple cider vinegar

1¼ cups superfine blanched almond flour

½ teaspoon salt

¼ teaspoon ground black pepper

1½ pounds boneless, skinless chicken breasts, cut into 2" strips no thicker than ½" (about 24 pieces)

Wasabi Ranch Dip
⅓ cup full-fat sour cream

2 tablespoons heavy whipping cream

½ tablespoon wasabi paste

½ tablespoon 100% lemon juice

½ tablespoon DLK House Ranch Dressing Mix (see recipe for Hurry Up House Salad with Ranch in Chapter 6)

¼ teaspoon ground black pepper

1 Line a large plate with paper towels.

2 In a large skillet over medium heat, heat oil until temperature reaches 350°F–375°F.

3 In a medium shallow bowl, combine mayonnaise and vinegar.

4 In a separate medium shallow bowl, combine almond flour, salt, and pepper.

5 Dredge chicken chunks first through the mayonnaise batter, coating all sides. Shake off any excess.

6 Next, rub all sides of chicken in almond flour mixture.

7 Add half of breaded chicken nuggets to hot oil and fry 2–3 minutes on each side until golden and cooked throughout. Repeat process for remaining nuggets. Place on lined plate to drain.

8 In a medium mixing bowl, whisk all Wasabi Ranch Dip ingredients together. Divide evenly among four dipping bowls.

9 Evenly distribute the nuggets onto four plates and serve each plate with bowl of dip. Serve warm.

TIPS & OPTIONS

Less adventurous palates might prefer homemade DLK House Ranch Dressing for dipping their chicken nuggets (see recipe for Hurry Up House Salad with Ranch in Chapter 6).

Random fact: Chicken nuggets are perfect for learning how to use chopsticks!

If you're looking for a sweeter dip, try rebooting leftover Barbecue Sauce from Close the Kitchen Early Quesadillas (see Chapter 7).

Prefer less mess? Preheat air fryer to 400°F and air-fry breaded chicken nuggets six at a time 10–12 minutes until fully cooked and golden, turning over halfway through.

LATE TO DINNER LASAGNA

I've learned to appreciate the merits of cabbage while on trips to Hawaii. It's readily used in place of lettuce because of cost and its ability to stay fresh for longer periods of time. In my community, a head of cabbage costs around a buck. *What a steal!* It's so versatile too. In this Late to Dinner Lasagna recipe, cabbage leaves replace noodles as a hearty, stable alternative.

1½ pounds Ready, Set, Go Ground Beef (see recipe in this chapter)

1 teaspoon minced garlic

2 cups no-sugar-added pasta sauce, divided

¼ teaspoon salt

⅛ teaspoon ground black pepper

2½ cups shredded whole milk mozzarella cheese, divided

1½ cups ricotta cheese

¼ cup grated Parmesan cheese

2 large eggs, beaten

2 teaspoons Italian seasoning

1 large head green cabbage, cored, leaves separated and steamed

1. Preheat oven to 375°F. Grease a 9" × 12" × 2" baking dish.

2. In a large skillet over medium heat, combine meat, garlic, 1½ cups pasta sauce, salt, and pepper and cook 5 minutes while stirring.

3. In a medium bowl, stir to combine 2 cups mozzarella, ricotta, Parmesan, eggs, and Italian seasoning until blended.

4. Evenly spread remaining ½ cup pasta sauce in prepared baking dish.

5. Layer half cabbage leaves next, no more than two leaves thick.

6. Evenly spread half of cheese mixture, followed by half of meat sauce.

7. Next, top with final cabbage layer, no more than two leaves thick. Follow with layer of remaining cheese mixture and remaining meat sauce.

8. Top with remaining ½ cup mozzarella.

9. Bake 15 minutes until cheese is starting to brown on top. Slice into ten servings and serve warm.

NET CARBS	
8G	

SERVES 10	
PER SERVING:	
CALORIES	356
FAT	18G
PROTEIN	34G
SODIUM	705MG
FIBER	4G
CARBOHYDRATES	12G
NET CARBS	8G
SUGAR	6G

TIME	
PREP TIME:	10 MINUTES
COOK TIME:	20 MINUTES
TOTAL TIME:	30 MINUTES

TIPS & OPTIONS

Leaves can be steamed or boiled. To boil, bring 4 cups water to a rolling boil in a large soup pot. Using metal tongs, dip cabbage leaves in boiling water a few at a time until they soften, 2–3 minutes.

Shop for marinara sauce wisely. Many brands contain added sugar! I prefer Hunt's Pasta Sauce No Added Sugar (from the dollar store!) or Rao's Homemade Marinara Sauce (found at local supermarkets, warehouse stores, and superstores).

HOT 'N' READY TINFOIL DINNER

NET CARBS

3G

SERVES 4

PER SERVING:

CALORIES	400
FAT	27G
PROTEIN	27G
SODIUM	527MG
FIBER	2G
CARBOHYDRATES	5G
NET CARBS	3G
SUGAR	2G

TIME

PREP TIME:	5 MINUTES
COOK TIME:	25 MINUTES
TOTAL TIME:	30 MINUTES

TIPS & OPTIONS

Suggested toppings are sour cream and bacon bits.

You could also substitute steak instead of chicken.

Kids love making Hot 'n' Ready Tinfoil Dinner. Encourage them to participate in making their individually wrapped dinner packets.

During winter, my children and I have cooked Hot 'n' Ready Tinfoil Dinner in our living room fireplace on the coals (Parental Supervision Required).

I spent countless summers of my youth around a campfire, both as a camper and later as a camp counselor. Not surprisingly, my favorite part of summer camp was the outdoor cooking. Planning the meals took a ton of work, especially for the little ones, and I had to find recipes that were simple to prepare and cook. Hot 'n' Ready Tinfoil Dinner fit the bill! You don't have to be camping or have a campfire to enjoy this meal. It's quick and easy to prepare on an outdoor grill.

> 5 tablespoons unsalted butter, melted
>
> 1½ tablespoons DLK House Ranch Dressing Mix (see recipe for Hurry Up House Salad with Ranch in Chapter 6)
>
> ¼ teaspoon salt
>
> ⅛ teaspoon ground black pepper
>
> 2 (8-ounce) bags radishes, trimmed and halved
>
> 1 pound boneless, skinless chicken thighs, diced into 1" chunks
>
> 1 cup shredded Cheddar cheese
>
> 1 tablespoon chopped fresh cilantro

1 Preheat an outdoor grill over medium heat. Grease four large pieces of foil with nonstick cooking spray.

2 In a small bowl, whisk together butter, DLK House Ranch Dressing Mix, salt, and pepper.

3 In a medium bowl, add radishes and top with half of butter mixture. Toss to coat.

4 Divide chicken and radish pieces evenly among the four pieces of foil. Top with remaining butter mixture.

5 Fold each piece of foil around chicken and radishes. Make sure it's sealed (double wrap if necessary) and cook on closed grill (or over campfire coals) 25 minutes until internal temperature is 170°F. Check regularly and stir to mix. Reduce heat if needed.

6 Transfer to four plates. Open packets, sprinkle with Cheddar and cilantro, and serve warm.

QUICKIE WEDDING CHICKEN

My friend Lori and I are ladies who lunch. Once a month, we venture out to gossip and eat delicious food together. We always claim to want to try new restaurants, but we end up going to the same place every time. Don't laugh, but we order the exact same dish too—Wedding Chicken! I think we would even lick the bowl if no one was looking. It's that good! Now you too can experience this dish. No reservations required, and ready in 30 minutes!

1 cup water, divided

½ cup full-fat cream cheese, softened

1 Grab and Go Chicken Breast, shredded (see recipe in this chapter)

1 (7-ounce) can chipotle peppers in adobo sauce, drained and finely chopped

2 (3.7-gram) chicken bouillon cubes

½ tablespoon xanthan gum

1. In a medium saucepan over medium heat, combine ¾ cup water and all remaining ingredients except xanthan gum.

2. Cook 15 minutes, stirring regularly until well combined.

3. In a medium bowl, whisk to combine remaining ¼ cup water and xanthan gum until thoroughly blended. Sprinkle xanthan gum mixture into saucepan slowly to prevent clumping.

4. Stir to thicken the Quickie Wedding Chicken for an additional 5 minutes.

5. Serve warm.

NET CARBS
5G

SERVES 4

PER SERVING:

CALORIES	171
FAT	9G
PROTEIN	7G
SODIUM	1,247MG
FIBER	7G
CARBOHYDRATES	12G
NET CARBS	5G
SUGAR	5G

TIME

PREP TIME:	10 MINUTES
COOK TIME:	20 MINUTES
TOTAL TIME:	30 MINUTES

TIPS & OPTIONS

I recommend serving Quickie Wedding Chicken with a hearty green salad. The rich sauce demands something lighter as a side dish, and chopped greens seems to pair perfectly.

If you have more time on your hands, you can also make this dish in a slow cooker. You don't need to chop the chipotle peppers using this method, because after a couple of hours cooking on low heat, the peppers all but disappear on their own into the Quickie Wedding Chicken sauce.

TWO-STEP SATAY WITH PEANUT SAUCE

NET CARBS

4G

SERVES 4

PER SERVING:

CALORIES	238
FAT	15G
PROTEIN	21G
SODIUM	405MG
FIBER	2G
CARBOHYDRATES	6G
NET CARBS	4G
SUGAR	1G

TIME

PREP TIME:	10 MINUTES
COOK TIME:	15 MINUTES
TOTAL TIME:	25 MINUTES

TIPS & OPTIONS

If using wooden skewers, soak them in water just prior to use to prevent skewers from burning on the grill.

To reduce carb count, substitute powdered peanut butter for regular no-sugar-added peanut butter. PBfit Peanut Butter Powder has 2 grams net carbs per 2-tablespoon serving compared to 6 grams net carbs per 2-tablespoon serving of Jif Creamy Peanut Butter. *Simply add water (and/or oil) and stir!*

My kids will eat just about anything when it's served in an unusual way, like how I prepare Two-Step Satay with Peanut Sauce. I like to mix it up, and skewers are an easy way to go. This tip might seem trivial, but I've found that variety (or lack thereof) affects my motivation to cook.

Two-Step Satay

2 (4.8-ounce) chicken breasts, cut in strips no thicker than ½" (make strips as uniform as possible)

6 ounces unsweetened canned full-fat coconut milk

1 tablespoon soy sauce

1 teaspoon minced garlic

½ teaspoon ground cumin

½ teaspoon ground ginger

½ teaspoon sesame seeds

Peanut Sauce

⅓ cup no-sugar-added creamy peanut butter

1½ tablespoons water

1 tablespoon soy sauce

½ tablespoon 100% lime juice

1 teaspoon white vinegar

1 teaspoon ground ginger

1 medium clove garlic, peeled and minced

4 (1-gram) packets 0g net carbs sweetener

1 Preheat outdoor grill over medium heat.

2 In a large Ziploc bag, place chicken and remaining Two-Step Satay ingredients except for sesame seeds. Squeeze out any air and seal the bag.

3 Knead bag to fully coat every chicken strip with seasonings. Put in the refrigerator to marinate while making Peanut Sauce.

4 In a medium bowl, whisk together all Peanut Sauce ingredients until mixed and sweetener is dissolved. If peanut butter is stiff, microwave covered sauce 10–20 seconds until softened and whisk again. Evenly divide sauce among four small bowls.

5 Divide chicken evenly into eight portions. Thread chicken pieces onto eight skewers.

6 Cook all skewers on the grill simultaneously 13–15 minutes, turning occasionally until golden.

7 Serve two skewers per plate. Sprinkle with sesame seeds and include a bowl of Peanut Sauce for dipping.

WIKIWIKI MAHI-MAHI

NET CARBS

1G

SERVES 4

PER SERVING:

CALORIES	340
FAT	27G
PROTEIN	22G
SODIUM	500MG
FIBER	0G
CARBOHYDRATES	1G
NET CARBS	1G
SUGAR	0G

TIME

PREP TIME:	10 MINUTES
COOK TIME:	12 MINUTES
TOTAL TIME:	22 MINUTES

TIPS & OPTIONS

If mahi-mahi fillets are not available in your community, substitute your favorite mild, firm fish. Suggestions include halibut, tuna, shark, or swordfish.

Save time and buy flash-frozen bags of individually portioned fish to keep on hand for dinners like Wikiwiki Mahi-Mahi. You can defrost only what you need and will always have the right ingredients on deck.

If you listen to my *DIRTY, LAZY, Girl* podcast, you'll remember that my New Year's resolution was to cook fresh fish once a week for dinner. My goal, however, might have been too aggressive. I don't always have time (or money!) to buy fresh fish fillets. Instead, I've modified my goal to include frozen fish. What really matters most to me is that I'm regularly eating delicious dinners like Wikiwiki Mahi-Mahi.

Fire Aioli

½ cup full-fat mayonnaise

2 teaspoons 100% lemon juice

½ teaspoon yellow mustard

1½ teaspoons minced garlic

¼ teaspoon salt

¼ teaspoon ground cayenne pepper

¼ teaspoon red pepper flakes

Mahi-Mahi Fillets

1 pound mahi-mahi fillets

⅛ teaspoon salt

⅛ teaspoon ground black pepper

2 tablespoons unsalted butter

1 In a medium bowl, whisk together all Fire Aioli ingredients until well blended. Cover and refrigerate until needed.

2 Lay fish fillets on a large plate and sprinkle both sides with salt and pepper.

3 In a large skillet over medium heat, melt butter. Add fillets so there is no overlapping and cook 4–6 minutes on each side until cooked throughout.

4 Divide fillets evenly among four dinner plates and top each with 2 tablespoons Fire Aioli. Serve.

ASIAN-INSPIRED TAKE-OUT TACOS

My days of ordering Chinese take-out are behind me. My standing order of sweet and sour chicken, cream cheese rangoons, and fried rice translates to carbs, carbs, *and oh, another side of carbs*. No more! I'm much happier (and thinner) eating an order of homemade Asian-Inspired Take-Out Tacos instead. I don't spend all day in the kitchen making this either. Time is on my side—I can knock out this meal in 30 minutes.

1 tablespoon unsalted butter

4 (4.2-ounce) boneless, skinless chicken breasts, cut in ¼" strips

1 teaspoon minced garlic

1½ teaspoons grated fresh ginger

1 tablespoon chopped green onion

2 tablespoons soy sauce

½ tablespoon rice vinegar

1 tablespoon peanut oil

¼ teaspoon red pepper flakes

10 drops liquid 0g net carbs sweetener

6 low-carb flour tortillas or reboot Tempo Tortillas (see Chapter 8)

1 In a large skillet over medium heat, melt butter. Add chicken, garlic, and ginger to skillet and cook 5–7 minutes, stirring until browned. Reduce heat to low.

2 Stir in remaining ingredients except tortillas. Cover and cook 15 minutes, stirring regularly.

3 Place 1 tortilla on each of six plates. Top each with one-sixth of meat mixture from the skillet. Serve warm.

NET CARBS

5G

SERVES 6

PER SERVING:

CALORIES	176
FAT	7G
PROTEIN	23G
SODIUM	602MG
FIBER	11G
CARBOHYDRATES	16G
NET CARBS	5G
SUGAR	0G

TIME

PREP TIME:	8 MINUTES
COOK TIME:	22 MINUTES
TOTAL TIME:	30 MINUTES

TIPS & OPTIONS

Make it a Pan-Asian theme night. Start today's meal with Thai Time Crunch Salad (see Chapter 6).

Serve a steaming side dish of low-carb Asian vegetables. Bok choy, mustard greens, or daikon come to mind.

RAPID-FIRE CHILI RELLENOS

Peppers scare my children. They have spent a lifetime watching their dad eat dangerously; he orders the spiciest food on any menu. *The hotter, the better!* No wonder my kids act suspicious when I start cooking poblano peppers to make Rapid-Fire Chili Rellenos. There is no convincing the little Laskas that dinner tonight is in fact quite mild and kid-friendly.

6 large whole poblano peppers

4 large eggs, beaten

⅔ cup green enchilada sauce

½ teaspoon salt

¼ teaspoon ground black pepper

1 pound Ready, Set, Go Ground Beef (see recipe in this chapter)

2 teaspoons taco seasoning mix

1 cup shredded Cheddar cheese

1 cup shredded Monterey jack cheese

¼ cup sliced black olives

1 Preheat oven to 425°F. Grease a 9" × 12" baking dish.

2 Turn all gas stovetop burners to medium-high heat.

3 Lay all peppers directly on flames (no pan). Cook peppers 1–2 minutes to completely char on all sides, using tongs to turn as needed.

4 Transfer hot charred peppers to a large Ziploc bag and seal 1 minute to steam and loosen charred skin.

5 In a medium bowl, whisk eggs, enchilada sauce, salt, and black pepper together.

6 Under cold water, remove charred skin from peppers and slice lengthwise. Remove stem, core, and seeds. Splay to create a single bottom layer in prepared baking dish.

7 In a medium skillet over medium heat, combine beef with seasoning mix. Stir 3–4 minutes until warm.

8 Top peppers with even layers of remaining ingredients: first Cheddar, then meat, egg mixture, Monterey jack, and finally olives.

9 Bake uncovered 16 minutes. Cover when browned to your satisfaction. Serve warm.

NET CARBS

5G

SERVES 9

PER SERVING:

CALORIES	279
FAT	15G
PROTEIN	25G
SODIUM	566MG
FIBER	3G
CARBOHYDRATES	8G
NET CARBS	5G
SUGAR	1G

TIME

PREP TIME:	5 MINUTES
COOK TIME:	25 MINUTES
TOTAL TIME:	30 MINUTES

TIPS & OPTIONS

Consider serving with Stopwatch Spanish "Rice" (see Chapter 9) as a side dish. *The more vegetables, the better, I say!*

Need a low-carb starter? Go for a theme night with Clip Chips and Salsa (see Chapter 7).

Don't have a gas stovetop? Char chiles under the broiler on high or outside on a barbecue. Even easier, you may substitute a can of drained diced green chile peppers for the bottom layer.

Chef's choice! Use red or green enchilada sauce, both 4 grams net carbs per ¼-cup serving.

CLOCK'S TICKIN' VODKA CHICKEN

TIPS & OPTIONS

Riced cauliflower will pair perfectly with this dish, giving you all the more tools to sop up the sauce.

Serve with Hurry Up House Salad with Ranch (see Chapter 6).

Mashed faux potatoes (made with cauliflower, cream, and salt) would also make a lovely side dish to accompany this.

The first time I made Clock's Tickin' Vodka Chicken I think I drank as much alcohol as was required for the recipe. I figured it would get me in the right mood for cooking. Not surprisingly, *it worked!* You don't have to have cocktails to enjoy this dish, however. Any added alcohol to the recipe is burned off during the cooking process. It's ready in under 30 minutes, looks pretty enough for company, and doesn't require much prep work. That's a triple win in my book!

1 tablespoon unsalted butter

1 tablespoon minced garlic

4 (4.2-ounce) boneless, skinless chicken breasts

¼ teaspoon salt

⅛ teaspoon ground black pepper

1 tablespoon finely chopped green onion

2 large eggs, beaten

1½ cups half and half

¼ cup 100% lemon juice

½ cup unflavored vodka

½ teaspoon Italian seasoning

½ teaspoon xanthan gum

1 tablespoon chopped fresh basil

1   In a large skillet over medium heat, melt butter. Add garlic, chicken, salt, and pepper and cook chicken 5–7 minutes on each side until browned.

2   Add remaining ingredients except xanthan gum and basil and stir until combined. Sprinkle in the xanthan gum slowly to prevent clumping and stir. Cover and cook 10 minutes, stirring regularly.

3   Serve warm on four dinner plates and top with fresh basil.

WARP-SPEED SAUSAGE AND SAUERKRAUT

Oktoberfest happens year-round at my house. I've never met a beer-drinking holiday that I didn't like! There are plenty of low-carb beers to choose from. Corona Premier, Michelob Ultra, and Miller Lite are a few of my favorites since they have only 3 grams net carbs per 12-ounce serving. I've learned to keep a cold brew in my hand while barbecuing German sausages. If the grill starts to flame up, a quick pour of beer extinguishes the fire with a side benefit of flavoring the meat. *Noch ein Bier, bitte!* (Another beer, please!)

> 4 uncooked German sausages (14 ounces total)
>
> 1 (12-ounce) bottle low-carb beer
>
> 1 tablespoon unsalted butter
>
> ½ cup sliced yellow onion
>
> 1 teaspoon minced garlic
>
> 16 ounces sauerkraut
>
> 1½ cups apple cider vinegar
>
> 1½ tablespoons 0g net carbs brown sugar substitute

1   Preheat outdoor grill to medium heat.

2   Grill sausages 15 minutes while turning until cooked. Don't forget to have your beer ready for flare-ups! Divide evenly among four plates.

3   In a large skillet over medium heat, melt butter. Add onion and garlic and brown 2 minutes while stirring.

4   Stir remaining ingredients into skillet and cook 8 minutes, stirring regularly.

5   Top sausages with sauerkraut mixture and serve warm.

NET CARBS

4G

SERVES 4

PER SERVING:

CALORIES	366
FAT	18G
PROTEIN	13G
SODIUM	1,595MG
FIBER	4G
CARBOHYDRATES	14G
NET CARBS	4G
SUGAR	3G
SUGAR ALCOHOL	6G

TIME

PREP TIME:	5 MINUTES
COOK TIME:	25 MINUTES
TOTAL TIME:	30 MINUTES

TIPS & OPTIONS

If outdoor grilling isn't an option, toss all of the ingredients into a slow cooker and walk away. Add washed and trimmed radishes to the pot while you're at it. With just 2 grams net carbs per 1-cup serving, radishes make a terrific baby potato substitute when "cooked to death" like inside a slow cooker. They pair perfectly with sausage and sauerkraut too!

GENERAL TSO'S SHORTCUT CHICKEN

TIPS & OPTIONS

General Tso's Shortcut Chicken can be served on a bed of riced cauliflower or salad greens.

Live a little. Serve with chopsticks!

Try sprinkling toasted sesame seeds on top just prior to serving for added flavor.

It's doubtful the *original* General Tso's Chicken was created in China (I'm guessing more like Panda Express!). I've cut the carbs from this popular takeout classic by using low-carb alternatives like almond flour for breading and sugar substitute to sweeten the sauce. These tricks are not an ancient Chinese secret. You too can learn to re-create old favorites.

Chicken

1½ pounds boneless, skinless chicken thighs, cubed

½ cup superfine blanched almond flour

2 large eggs, beaten

1 teaspoon minced garlic

¼ teaspoon salt

⅛ teaspoon ground black pepper

½ teaspoon xanthan gum

2 cups vegetable oil

Sauce

¼ cup soy sauce

¼ cup chicken broth

2 tablespoons 0g net carbs sweetener

1 tablespoon minced garlic

½ teaspoon red pepper flakes

¼ teaspoon ground ginger

2 teaspoons sesame seeds

1 In a large resealable bag, add all Chicken ingredients except xanthan gum and oil. Seal and shake until all chicken is coated with seasoning. Sprinkle xanthan gum in slowly to prevent clumping and shake the sealed bag again to thoroughly coat.

2 Line a large plate with paper towels.

3 In a large skillet over medium heat, heat oil. Carefully add chicken and fry 7–10 minutes, turning until golden.

4 Remove chicken to lined plate.

5 In a large bowl, whisk all Sauce ingredients together.

6 In a clean large skillet over medium heat, add Chicken and Sauce and cook 10 minutes, stirring regularly.

7 Evenly serve warm on six dinner plates.

BARELY ANY WORK BEEF AND BROCCOLI BOWL

Sometimes I overthink dinner. I stand in front of the fridge with both doors wide open in a complete daze. It's like I'm hoping the food will shout out a dinner idea to me. This has yet to happen, but I keep trying the technique. *Am I alone?* If you too find yourself in a refrigerator stupor, remember these two words: *Beef* and *Broccoli*. These bowls are simple, easy to make, and will please everyone in your family.

1 tablespoon olive oil

1 pound skirt steak, thinly sliced

¼ cup soy sauce

1 teaspoon 100% lime juice

2 tablespoons 0g net carbs brown sugar substitute

2 teaspoons minced garlic

1 teaspoon ground ginger

¼ teaspoon ground black pepper

3 cups bite-sized broccoli florets

¼ cup chopped green onion

1 teaspoon sesame seeds

1 In a medium skillet over medium heat, heat oil.

2 Add steak and cook 10 minutes, stirring regularly.

3 In a medium bowl, whisk together soy sauce, lime juice, brown sugar substitute, garlic, ginger, and pepper. Add broccoli and toss to coat completely. Stir this mixture into skillet. Cook an additional 10 minutes while stirring.

4 Serve warm topped with a sprinkle of green onion and sesame seeds.

NET CARBS

4G

SERVES 4

PER SERVING:

CALORIES	245
FAT	13G
PROTEIN	24G
SODIUM	85MG
FIBER	2G
CARBOHYDRATES	12G
NET CARBS	4G
SUGAR	2G
SUGAR ALCOHOL	6G

TIME

PREP TIME:	10 MINUTES
COOK TIME:	20 MINUTES
TOTAL TIME:	30 MINUTES

TIPS & OPTIONS

Other than skirt, my recommended cuts of steak to use here are hanger or flank steak.

Are you trying to cut back on eating red meat? Chicken, pork, or even shrimp would make a nice substitute here.

CHAPTER 11

DRINKS AND DESSERTS

Can a drink or dessert ever be too sweet? My answer, sadly, is *no*. Food can never be sweet enough. I don't think I've ever spit out a sip of sweet tea for having too much sugar or turned away a piece of strawberry pie for having too much glaze. Who does that? Not me! I was always the one adding "just a little more sugar" to get the sweetness level up to the big leagues…*to cavity level*!

No wonder my taste buds are so warped! Surely I wasn't born this way. When I look back at pictures from my childhood, though, I start to learn clues that might explain my lifetime addiction to sweets. As a toddler, my bottles were filled with bright-red "bug juice." I could barely walk or talk, but I recognized the dancing pitcher of punch on television busting through a wall. That was my hero, the Kool-Aid Man.

It seems I was doomed from the start. To complicate things further, when I craved sweets, I became impatient. I would reach for the first sugary option within reach.

My addiction to sugar went on for decades. From chocolate milk in the hot lunch line to chasing the ice cream truck down the block after school let out, I couldn't get enough. Mentally, I knew sugary drinks and desserts contributed to my weight problem, but still, I couldn't stop consuming them. Go cold turkey? No way. For me, that's never been a realistic option. I suspect you, too, might relate.

DIRTY, LAZY, KETO has been a godsend. I finally figured out a way I could make my sugar-free cake *and eat it too!* And the best part? I learned how to make substitute treats FAST. I'm able to enjoy modified desserts or drinks with flavors I'm used to without a lot of fuss in the kitchen. I don't feel deprived or resentful for having to give up my favorite foods. Instead, I quickly whip up a DLK version to enjoy in minutes flat.

When you know better, you do better. It may have taken me a really long time, but I've finally arrived.

SWOOP CREAM ↻ ◊ ✕ ✎

It's almost comical how excited people get when they find out that whipped cream is DLK-approved. They become giddy with excitement. It doesn't matter how old you are; everyone loves to stand in front of the refrigerator and squirt whipped cream into their mouth, straight from the can. I don't know if it's due to the can or the taste, but even dogs are getting in on the game (*I'll have a Puppuccino, please!*). It's time to class up our act, people. Let's stop eating from the can and make a proper dish of Swoop Cream.

1 cup heavy whipping cream

¼ teaspoon 0g net carbs liquid sweetener

½ teaspoon pure vanilla extract

1 In a medium bowl of an electric mixer, whip all ingredients on high speed 1–2 minutes until soft peaks form.

2 Serve cool.

NET CARBS	
1G	
SERVES 8	
PER SERVING:	
CALORIES	103
FAT	10G
PROTEIN	1G
SODIUM	11MG
FIBER	0G
CARBOHYDRATES	1G
NET CARBS	1G
SUGAR	1G

TIME	
PREP TIME:	10 MINUTES
COOK TIME:	0 MINUTES
TOTAL TIME:	10 MINUTES

TIPS & OPTIONS

Chill the electric beater attachment and mixing bowl first (at least 30 minutes in the refrigerator or 10 minutes in the freezer) to create a longer-lasting Swoop Cream.

Swoop Cream doesn't have to go solo. Use your imagination here… Just like they do at a coffee shop, sprinkle a dusting of cocoa powder, cinnamon, or even crushed (sugar-free) candy on top for added flair.

Reboot leftover Swoop Cream to top fresh berries, hot cocoa, or even a smoothie.

STAMPEDE STRAWBERRY MILKSHAKE

I could easily eat a pound of strawberries in one sitting. After all, they're a "low sugar" fruit, right? *Yes and no.* A serving of strawberries has 8 grams net carbs, but that's just for 1 cup. The plastic clamshells that many of us buy at the supermarket hold a pound of strawberries—that translates to 2¾ cups, or 22 grams net carbs. Bottom line? The net carbs add up fast. Instead of eating a bowl of berries by themselves, I use them as a topping (or an ingredient that I can measure), as in Stampede Strawberry Milkshake.

1 cup crushed ice cubes

½ cup sliced strawberries, divided

¼ cup heavy whipping cream

1 tablespoon full-fat cream cheese, softened

2 cups unsweetened vanilla almond milk

1 scoop low-carb vanilla protein powder

1 teaspoon pure vanilla extract

4 (1-gram) packets 0g net carbs sweetener

1   In a blender, add ice, then remaining ingredients, holding back 2 strawberry slices, and blend 1–2 minutes until creamy.

2   Divide evenly between two tall glasses. Garnish each glass with 1 strawberry slice. Serve immediately.

TIPS & OPTIONS

Unless I catch an amazing sale, I tend to stick with Premier Protein or Quest brand low-carb protein powders. They both come in a variety of flavors, but I find the vanilla and chocolate flavors to be the easiest to work with.

Want to substitute frozen strawberries for fresh? *You got it.* Reduce the amount of ice—and maybe add more liquid to compensate (or risk burning out your blender's motor).

As always, every drink looks and tastes better when presented with a dollop of homemade Swoop Cream on top (see recipe in this chapter).

BUSY BEE BLUEBERRY SMOOTHIE

NET CARBS

9G

SERVES 1

PER SERVING:

CALORIES	328
FAT	19G
PROTEIN	27G
SODIUM	360MG
FIBER	3G
CARBOHYDRATES	12G
NET CARBS	9G
SUGAR	7G

TIME

PREP TIME:	3 MINUTES
COOK TIME:	0 MINUTES
TOTAL TIME:	3 MINUTES

TIPS & OPTIONS

Instead of heavy whipping cream, try an avocado.

Frozen or fresh blueberries? Either will do.

When using protein powder, I recommend Quest or Premier Protein brands. Quest comes in a variety of flavors, but Premier Protein offers both liquid (ready to drink) and powder formulations.

I like sneaking spinach into my smoothies. I forget it's even there! But if the vegetable flavor bothers you (or gets caught up in your reusable straw), feel free to omit this ingredient.

Busy morning tomorrow? No excuses! Assemble the Busy Bee Blueberry Smoothie ingredients right now while you still have the motivation (which we all know can be fleeting at the crack of dawn!). Add the dry ingredients to your blender and refrigerate the whole kit and caboodle until tomorrow. When you wake up, add the ice and liquids and blend. Your homemade Busy Bee Blueberry Smoothie will be tastier, quicker, and certainly healthier than any trip to a drive-thru.

> 1 cup ice cubes
> ¼ cup blueberries
> 1 cup spinach
> 1 cup unsweetened vanilla almond milk
> 1 scoop berry-flavored low-carb protein powder
> 3 tablespoons heavy whipping cream
> ½ teaspoon pure vanilla extract
> 4 (1-gram) packets 0g net carbs sweetener

1 In a blender, add ice, then remaining ingredients.

2 Pulse 1–2 minutes until desired consistency is reached.

3 Serve immediately.

COMMUTER CARAMEL MACCHIATO

I have a very good friend who visits Starbucks every day (well, twice a day if we're being 100 percent honest!). That kind of regime takes commitment, not to mention a lot of time in your car. Myself? I'd rather brew up a quick Commuter Caramel Macchiato at home. It's affordable, faster, and there's never a line. I have all the tools I need to be an expert barista. Just like Starbucks, I keep a clear set of salt and pepper shakers next to my coffee pot, one full of cinnamon, the other, powdered cocoa. Dress up your coffee, but do it on the cheap.

14 ounces brewed macchiato, hot and unsweetened

¼ cup heavy whipping cream

½ teaspoon pure vanilla extract

1 (1-gram) packet 0g net carbs sweetener

2 tablespoons sugar-free caramel syrup

1 Add all ingredients to a blender and pulse 15–30 seconds to blend.

2 Serve immediately in two coffee mugs while still hot.

NET CARBS

5G

SERVES 2

PER SERVING:	
CALORIES	125
FAT	11G
PROTEIN	1G
SODIUM	41MG
FIBER	0G
CARBOHYDRATES	5G
NET CARBS	5G
SUGAR	1G

TIME

PREP TIME:	3 MINUTES
COOK TIME:	0 MINUTES
TOTAL TIME:	3 MINUTES

TIPS & OPTIONS

Serve over ice for a refreshing summer treat.

Torani makes all sorts of fun sugar-free flavored syrups.

Heavy whipping cream is a common culprit behind a weight loss stall. If you find that the needle on the scale stops moving, take a close look at how much cream you're actually consuming.

Instead of getting your blender dirty, invest in an inexpensive handheld immersion blender. It's a much faster cleanup (just rinse and dry), but mostly, *it's fun to froth*!

PACE YOURSELF PIÑA COLADA

I'm a multitasker with busy fingers. In fact, it's impossible for me to just sit and do nothing at all. I need something for my idle hands to do or else I start reaching for food (and I'm not even hungry!). Much to my family's chagrin, I decided to pick up the ukulele. Strumming this simple instrument keeps me out of the popcorn bowl and calms me down more than any snack ever could. I'm immediately transported to happy memories from past vacations. One of the first songs I learned to play is, you guessed it, "Escape (The Piña Colada Song)"!

1½ cups ice

½ teaspoon Sugar-Free Pineapple Drink Enhancer

1 cup unsweetened canned coconut milk (12–14% coconut fat)

1 (1½-ounce) shot unflavored white rum

1 teaspoon 100% lemon juice

4 whole raspberries

2 green leaves from a pineapple crown

1 In a blender, add ice, then remaining ingredients except raspberries and pineapple leaves.

2 Pulse 1–2 minutes until desired consistency is reached, adding water if needed. Divide evenly between two tall glasses.

3 Using a toothpick, pierce two raspberries and one pineapple leaf. Balance garnish on lip of glass. Repeat for second glass. Serve immediately.

NET CARBS
2G

SERVES 2	
PER SERVING:	
CALORIES	199
FAT	15G
PROTEIN	2G
SODIUM	60MG
FIBER	0G
CARBOHYDRATES	2G
NET CARBS	2G
SUGAR	0G

TIME	
PREP TIME:	3 MINUTES
COOK TIME:	0 MINUTES
TOTAL TIME:	3 MINUTES

TIPS & OPTIONS

For a Virgin Pace Yourself Piña Colada, omit the rum.

There is no need to buy an actual pineapple for this recipe. Simply pluck two leaves off of one of the fruits in the store and call it a day.

If you don't have canned coconut milk on hand, substitute 2 tablespoons Swoop Cream (see recipe in this chapter) and 1 cup unsweetened, unflavored coconut milk from a carton.

An alternate source of pineapple flavoring is Jordan's Skinny Syrups Pineapple or Torani Sugar Free Pineapple Syrup.

SNAPPY AND SWEET ICED TEA

TIPS & OPTIONS

Adjust the tea, lemonade, and sweetener levels to suit your tastes.

Get crazy and use lime slices in addition to (or in place of) the lemon slices. The vitamin C will do you good.

Don't forget to wash the lemon or lime before you slice it. The outer peel will be in your beverage, after all.

I used to drink Diet Coke at every meal—*even breakfast*! Nowadays, I keep a twelve-pack in the garage (which lasts for a month). I tell myself I can "still have it," of course, but having to walk *allllllllll the way to the garage* (followed by a trip to the fridge for a cup of ice) is often too much of a hassle. I did this on purpose, you see. Making diet soda inconvenient pushes me to drink caffeine-free beverages like a glass of Snappy and Sweet Iced Tea. I keep a pitcher cold inside the fridge.

4 cups unsweetened brewed herbal tea, chilled

4 cups sugar-free lemonade, chilled

3 (1-gram) packets 0g net carbs sweetener

8 thin slices lemon

1 In a pitcher, add all ingredients and stir to combine until sweetener is dissolved.

2 Divide evenly among four tall glasses and serve immediately while still chilled.

MAMA'S MOVIN' FAST FUDGE

I spent the summers of my youth visiting Mackinac Island, Michigan, the fudge capital of the United States, so I consider myself to be a trained expert. (There was a lot of fudge eating on those vacations, you see!) Mama's Movin' Fast Fudge recipe ranks right up there with the best of them. I don't keep whole milk on hand much these days, but when I'm craving my Mama's Movin' Fast Fudge, I make an exception. A half-pint is all you'll need from the store to whip up the most amazing dessert.

2 cups unsweetened 100% cocoa powder

¾ cup unsalted butter, softened

1 cup water

⅔ cup whole milk

1 cup 0g net carbs sweetener

1 teaspoon pure vanilla extract

¼ teaspoon salt

1   Grease a 9" × 9" baking dish.

2   In the top pan of a double boiler add cocoa powder and butter, and stir to combine.

3   In the bottom pan of the double boiler add water and bring to a boil over medium-high heat. Reduce heat to low and cover with the top pan.

4   Stir cocoa mixture constantly while slowly adding milk, sweetener, vanilla, and salt until fudge is completely blended and creamy, approximately 10 minutes. Fudge will become increasingly more difficult to stir.

5   Transfer fudge to prepared baking dish. Using a spatula, evenly press fudge into all corners of the dish. Cover and refrigerate.

6   Serve cold. Cut into serving-sized squares right before serving.

NET CARBS
2G

SERVES 20

PER SERVING:

CALORIES	90
FAT	8G
PROTEIN	2G
SODIUM	35MG
FIBER	3G
CARBOHYDRATES	10G
NET CARBS	2G
SUGAR	1G
SUGAR ALCOHOL	5G

TIME

PREP TIME:	15 MINUTES
COOK TIME:	10 MINUTES
TOTAL TIME:	25 MINUTES

TIPS & OPTIONS

Take extra precaution while stirring the hot cocoa and butter mixture in the double boiler. Steam is escaping from the bottom pan of the double boiler.

Once cooled, cut fudge into individually sized portions of 2" × 2" squares. (Recipe makes approximately twenty pieces of candy.) Place immediately into snack-sized Ziploc bags or else risk overindulging!

Hide fudge in the very bottom of your freezer, away from yourself and others. Keep for when an emergency chocolate craving occurs.

HIBISCUS TURBO TEA

NET CARBS

2G

SERVES 4

PER SERVING:

CALORIES	66
FAT	6G
PROTEIN	1G
SODIUM	26MG
FIBER	0G
CARBOHYDRATES	2G
NET CARBS	2G
SUGAR	0G

TIME

PREP TIME:	10 MINUTES
COOK TIME:	0 MINUTES
TOTAL TIME:	10 MINUTES

TIPS & OPTIONS ⟫

Adjust the tea, coconut milk, and sweetener levels to suit your tastes.

Trick your friends into believing you just came from Starbucks with a Pink Drink—float slices of strawberry inside your drink and serve in a recycled clear cup with lid.

I was at a work meeting the first time I tried a cup of hibiscus tea. I was feeling jittery from all the coffee I had been drinking that morning, so I decided to try a lighter alternative. Maybe it was due to its gorgeous pink color, but I fell in love with this new brew on the spot. The flavor is somewhat tart, almost like what you'd taste biting into a fresh cranberry. To remedy that sour flavor, I add coconut milk and sugar-free sweetener. The combination makes the most delicious cup of Hibiscus Turbo Tea.

6 cups unsweetened brewed hibiscus tea

¾ cup unsweetened canned coconut milk, Premium 12–14% coconut fat

6 (1-gram) packets 0g net carbs sweetener

2 teaspoons pure vanilla extract

1½ cups ice cubes

¼ cup fresh mint leaves

1   Add tea, coconut milk, sweetener, and vanilla to a pitcher and stir to combine until sweetener is dissolved.

2   Divide evenly among four tall glasses over ice. Top with mint leaves and serve.

CAYENNE CHARGED CHOCOLATE PUDDING

NET CARBS

6G

SERVES 2

PER SERVING:
CALORIES	299
FAT	24G
PROTEIN	4G
SODIUM	159MG
FIBER	12G
CARBOHYDRATES	18G
NET CARBS	6G
SUGAR	2G

TIME

PREP TIME:	10 MINUTES
COOK TIME:	0 MINUTES
TOTAL TIME:	10 MINUTES

TIPS & OPTIONS ≫

If you must, omit the cayenne. Maybe next time you'll be braver.

The avocados MUST be at peak ripeness. This is required for them to blend properly and create the thick "fat" base needed for Cayenne Charged Chocolate Pudding.

I've never met a pudding I didn't like. I'm sure Freud would point back to my toddler days as an explanation, but for me, I just love creamy food on a spoon. Yogurt, soups, or pudding? I love them all. Cayenne Charged Chocolate Pudding is definitely for grown folks, though. There is no kid play when it comes to the kick of cayenne!

3 tablespoons unsweetened canned coconut milk

2 medium avocados, peeled and pitted

½ cup ice cubes

2 tablespoons unsweetened 100% cocoa powder

1 teaspoon pure vanilla extract

1 teaspoon ground cinnamon

2 tablespoons 0g net carbs sweetener

⅛ teaspoon salt

⅛ teaspoon ground cayenne pepper

1   Add all ingredients to a food processor or blender and pulse until even and creamy, 2–3 minutes, stopping midway to scrape down sides with a rubber spatula.

2   Serve immediately.

BREAKNECK SALTY PECAN BARK

Craving chocolate doesn't make you a DLK flunky. Desiring sweets is normal. Instead of flogging yourself for wanting a dessert, figure out how to satisfy your urge (*oooh, that sounds scandalous!*). Some folks find success by keeping a dark chocolate gourmet candy bar (in the freezer) for a nip. Would that work for you—*or would you eat the whole bar?* It's the age-old conundrum of quality versus quantity. Myself, I prefer a few pieces of sugar-free Breakneck Salty Pecan Bark.

1 cup sugar-free chocolate chips

1 tablespoon coconut oil

1 cup pecan halves

⅛ teaspoon salt

1   Line a small baking sheet with parchment paper.

2   In a medium microwave-safe bowl, add chocolate chips and oil and microwave on high 30 seconds. Stir and microwave again 30 seconds.

3   Stir in pecans until coated.

4   Spread mixture evenly on prepared baking sheet (one that will fit in your freezer). Sprinkle with salt.

5   Freeze at least 20 minutes to harden.

6   Break into 1"–2" pieces and serve. Store leftovers in a medium resealable container.

NET CARBS	
2G	

SERVES 6	
PER SERVING:	
CALORIES	276
FAT	24G
PROTEIN	4G
SODIUM	48MG
FIBER	11G
CARBOHYDRATES	21G
NET CARBS	2G
SUGAR	1G
SUGAR ALCOHOL	8G

TIME	
PREP TIME:	25 MINUTES
COOK TIME:	1 MINUTE
TOTAL TIME:	26 MINUTES

 TIPS & OPTIONS

Any type of nut can be used in this recipe. Experiment with other low-carb nuts such as hazelnuts, almonds, or macadamia nuts (all 2 grams net carbs per 1-ounce serving).

Double up on this recipe so you have plenty. This tasty and simple dessert won't last long, especially when word gets out.

Dip chunks of Breakneck Salty Pecan Bark into peanut butter. *You're welcome.*

FRENZIED UNICORN FRAP

My teenage children can be bribed to do just about anything with the promise of a trip to Starbucks afterward. I'm always surprised by what they order. It's never on the menu, but the employees know exactly what they want. Apparently, I'm too old to know about the secret menu. I created this low-carb version of their favorite drink, the Unicorn Frappuccino, just so they would stop calling me a "boomer."

> 2 cups ice cubes
>
> 1½ cups unsweetened vanilla almond milk
>
> 3 tablespoons 0g net carbs sweetener
>
> ½ teaspoon pure vanilla extract
>
> ½ cup blueberries plus 8 whole fresh berries, divided
>
> ¼ cup Swoop Cream (see recipe in this chapter)
>
> 1 tablespoon sugar-free strawberry syrup

1. To a blender add ice, almond milk, sweetener, vanilla, and ½ cup blueberries. Pulse 30–60 seconds to blend.

2. Divide evenly between two tall glasses. Top each glass with 2 tablespoons Swoop Cream. Evenly drizzle strawberry syrup on top of cream.

3. Thread four blueberries onto a cocktail skewer; repeat with remaining blueberries. Garnish drinks with skewers and serve immediately.

NET CARBS

6G

SERVES 2

PER SERVING:

CALORIES	101
FAT	7G
PROTEIN	2G
SODIUM	151MG
FIBER	2G
CARBOHYDRATES	8G
NET CARBS	6G
SUGAR	5G

TIME

PREP TIME:	10 MINUTES
COOK TIME:	0 MINUTES
TOTAL TIME:	10 MINUTES

TIPS & OPTIONS

Fresh or frozen blueberries can be used.

If you are like me and struggle with not being one of the "cool kids," search for upcoming trends using #starbuckssecretmenu on *Instagram*. At the very least, you can name-drop the newest drinks and impress the grandkids. Don't have *Instagram*? Hmmm… Well, maybe I can't help you after all.

PER SERVING:

CALORIES	100
FAT	6G
PROTEIN	8G
SODIUM	401MG
FIBER	5G
CARBOHYDRATES	7G
NET CARBS	2G
SUGAR	0G

TIME

PREP TIME:	15 SECONDS
COOK TIME:	45 SECONDS
TOTAL TIME:	1 MINUTE

TIPS & OPTIONS

Always make sure you have your food covered when heating in the microwave. It has a tendency to splatter and boil all over the place at times.

In moments of weakness, I've convinced myself it's acceptable to double or triple this recipe (don't judge). Let me forewarn you: This never ends well.

BEEP, BEEP, BROWNIE!

I have serious problems when it comes to portion control. It's like my mind sees a pan of brownies and thinks to itself, "One pan equals one serving for me!" If low-carb desserts are in the house, I nibble away at them until they're gone, one bite at a time, every time I pass through the kitchen. Making single-serving-sized desserts like Beep, Beep, Brownie!, cooked in the microwave in just a minute, has truly been a godsend. I enjoy eating this without any guilt or worry about going overboard.

1 large egg

1 tablespoon unsweetened 100% cocoa powder

1 tablespoon 0g net carbs sweetener

1 tablespoon Carbquik baking mix

⅛ teaspoon pure vanilla extract

⅛ teaspoon salt

1 In a well-greased coffee mug, beat egg with a fork.

2 Add remaining ingredients and stir thoroughly to combine.

3 Microwave on high covered 45 seconds. Enjoy warm right from mug.

FRANTIC VANILLA FROSTING

Frosting makes everything tastes better; wouldn't you agree? I created Frantic Vanilla Frosting out of necessity. I desperately wanted something sweet but hadn't been to the grocery store yet that week. I was out of, well, almost everything. With only a few dribs and drabs in every container, I mixed and matched, blended and creamed. The resulting mixture was a frosting recipe worthy of posting in the DLK Hall of Fame. Frantic Vanilla Frosting can be enjoyed on any dessert (or more often than not at my house, simply licked off a spoon).

> 3 tablespoons full-fat cream cheese, softened
>
> 1½ tablespoons heavy whipping cream
>
> 2 tablespoons 0g net carbs sweetener
>
> ¼ teaspoon pure vanilla extract

1   In a small bowl, blend all ingredients until smooth. If desired, use an electric hand mixer to smooth out any lumps.

2   Cover and refrigerate until ready to serve. Eat within four days.

NET CARBS

1G

SERVES 8

PER SERVING:

CALORIES	23
FAT	2G
PROTEIN	0G
SODIUM	20MG
FIBER	0G
CARBOHYDRATES	3G
NET CARBS	1G
SUGAR	0G
SUGAR ALCOHOL	2G

TIME

PREP TIME:	2 MINUTES
COOK TIME:	0 MINUTES
TOTAL TIME:	2 MINUTES

TIPS & OPTIONS

Frantically whisk the frosting by hand and avoid having to get out the mixer. You can do it!

Add a few drops of food coloring to your frosting to magically customize any dessert.

Reboot Frantic Vanilla Frosting with a variety of recipes: Swift Cinnamon Rolls (see Chapter 5), Shortcut Cinnamon Toast Sticks (see Chapter 5), Delivery Donuts (see Chapter 5), or Avocado Bolt Brownies (see recipe in this chapter), just to name a few.

CRASH COURSE CHOCOLATE CHIP COOKIES

NET CARBS

2G

SERVES 8

PER SERVING:

CALORIES	231
FAT	21G
PROTEIN	5G
SODIUM	24MG
FIBER	3G
CARBOHYDRATES	9G
NET CARBS	2G
SUGAR	1G
SUGAR ALCOHOL	4G

TIME

PREP TIME:	10 MINUTES
COOK TIME:	20 MINUTES
TOTAL TIME:	30 MINUTES

TIPS & OPTIONS

If you choose, add a different low-carb nut prior to mixing. Might I suggest walnuts?

Live a little. Fold pieces of Atkins Endulge Chocolate Peanut Candies (which look like M&M's) into the batter prior to baking. They have just 1 gram net carbs per 1 (1.2-ounce) pack serving.

Use room-temperature butter and cream cheese for this recipe (avoid using the microwave, which could oversoften it). This little tip will prevent your cookies from turning into melted pancakes.

My first few attempts at creating these family favorites resulted in a giant mess. My cookies were either too puffy, or worse, melted into one giant puddle. Ironically, my family didn't care one bit. (Truth be told, neither did I!) We were usually so excited to have homemade Crash Course Chocolate Chip Cookies coming out of the oven that we paid little attention to their unique shape.

1¼ cups superfine blanched almond flour

3½ tablespoons full-fat cream cheese, softened

¼ cup unsalted butter, softened

¼ cup 0g net carbs sweetener

½ teaspoon pure vanilla extract

¼ cup whole macadamia nuts

2 tablespoons sugar-free chocolate chips

1 Preheat oven to 350°F. Line a baking sheet with parchment paper.

2 In a medium bowl, combine all ingredients except nuts and chocolate chips. Stir until thoroughly mixed and a dough forms.

3 Fold in nuts and chocolate chips until evenly incorporated.

4 Scoop out dough in 1" balls and pat down to no more than ¼" thickness. Place on parchment paper with at least ½" between cookies.

5 Bake 20 minutes until cookies start to brown.

6 Transfer to a plate and serve warm.

INSTANT ICE CREAM

My addiction to sweet and salty foods probably started when I was in preschool. I remember dipping French fries into a paper-wrapped ice cream cone and thinking I should call Ronald McDonald to tell him my discovery. Nowadays, I sub zucchini fries or salty green beans for my fry fix, and Instant Ice Cream for the occasional dessert treat.

¾ cup frozen sliced unsweetened strawberries

¾ cup heavy whipping cream, very cold

6 (1-gram) packets 0g net carbs sweetener

1 In a food processor, add all ingredients and pulse 30–60 seconds until smooth and thick.

2 Divide between two chilled bowls and serve immediately.

NET CARBS

7G

SERVES 2

PER SERVING:

CALORIES	327
FAT	31G
PROTEIN	2G
SODIUM	34MG
FIBER	1G
CARBOHYDRATES	8G
NET CARBS	7G
SUGAR	5G

TIME

PREP TIME:	5 MINUTES
COOK TIME:	0 MINUTES
TOTAL TIME:	5 MINUTES

TIPS & OPTIONS

Heavy whipping cream, the key ingredient in keto ice cream, should be enjoyed in moderation. Even though the ingredient has low (or no) carbs per serving, cream is calorie dense. All of that deliciousness is easy to overdo! That's why dairy is toward the top of the DIRTY, LAZY, KETO food pyramid.

BYE-BYE BACON MAPLE CUPCAKES

One of the many things I love about a cupcake is its size—*built-in portion control*. The next time you're craving a salty-sweet treat, whip up a quick batch of these low-carb bacon maple beauties.

Cupcakes

½ cup unsalted butter, softened

1 cup full-fat cream cheese, softened

1 cup 0g net carbs sweetener

1 teaspoon pure vanilla extract

2 tablespoons sugar-free pancake syrup

4 large eggs

1 tablespoon baking powder

½ teaspoon salt

2½ cups superfine blanched almond flour

Maple Frosting

1 cup unsalted butter, softened

1½ cups 0g net carbs confectioners'-style sweetener

3 tablespoons heavy whipping cream

3 tablespoons sugar-free pancake syrup, divided

¼ cup cooked bacon bits

½ cup pecan halves

1 Preheat oven to 375°F. Line twenty cups of two muffin tins with twenty cupcake liners.

2 In the medium bowl of an electric mixer, combine butter, cream cheese, sweetener, vanilla, syrup, and eggs. Beat on high speed until batter is smooth. Add baking powder and salt. Beat again, scraping sides of bowl often.

3 Add almond flour and beat until thoroughly combined.

4 Divide batter equally among prepared muffin cups.

5 Bake 20 minutes until a toothpick inserted into the center of a cupcake comes out clean. Let cool 3 minutes. Remove cupcakes from tins to a cooling rack.

6 In a small bowl, mix butter, confectioners'-style sweetener, cream, and 2 teaspoons syrup and beat 2–3 minutes until thoroughly combined.

7 Place frosting into a piping bag and pipe Maple Frosting onto cupcakes, leaving liners on. Evenly sprinkle bacon bits and pecans on cupcakes. Drizzle with remaining syrup.

8 Serve or store in an airtight container in the refrigerator.

NET CARBS	
2G	

SERVES 20	
PER SERVING:	
CALORIES	299
FAT	28G
PROTEIN	6G
SODIUM	232MG
FIBER	2G
CARBOHYDRATES	15G
NET CARBS	2G
SUGAR	1G
SUGAR ALCOHOL	11G

TIME	
PREP TIME:	10 MINUTES
COOK TIME:	20 MINUTES
TOTAL TIME:	30 MINUTES

TIPS & OPTIONS

You can make your own sugar-free confectioners'-style sweetener by blending the sweetener of your choice in a high-speed blender with just a pinch of cornstarch. (For your reference, cornstarch has 7 grams net carbs per 1-tablespoon serving.)

Instead of a fancy-pants pastry bag, I use a heavy-duty, gallon-sized Ziploc bag with the corner snipped off. The cleanup is much faster this way! Simply toss the bag when finished.

AVOCADO BOLT BROWNIES

Similar to the draw of popcorn at the movie theater, something magical happens when homemade brownies bake in the oven. Granted, I'm assuming your Avocado Bolt Brownies actually make it into the oven! Just this morning as I was making a batch of these gems, my daughter had to pull the pan away from me as I kept sticking my tasting spatula back into the batter. (Oh, don't act like you haven't done that!)

2 medium avocados, peeled, pitted, and mashed

2 large eggs, beaten

⅓ cup unsweetened 100% cocoa powder

⅓ cup superfine blanched almond flour

¾ cup 0g net carbs brown sugar substitute

1 teaspoon pure vanilla extract

1 teaspoon baking powder

¼ teaspoon salt

½ cup sugar-free chocolate chips

1 Preheat oven to 350°F. Grease a 9″ × 9″ baking dish.

2 In a food processor or blender, add all ingredients except chocolate chips. Blend 2–3 minutes until creamy, scraping batter from the sides often.

3 Fold in chocolate chips and pour into prepared baking dish. Bake 25 minutes until a toothpick inserted in the center comes out clean.

4 Slice into twelve servings. Serve warm.

NET CARBS

3G

SERVES 12

PER SERVING:

CALORIES	109
FAT	9G
PROTEIN	3G
SODIUM	103MG
FIBER	5G
CARBOHYDRATES	22G
NET CARBS	3G
SUGAR	0G
SUGAR ALCOHOL	14G

TIME

PREP TIME:	5 MINUTES
COOK TIME:	25 MINUTES
TOTAL TIME:	30 MINUTES

TIPS & OPTIONS

Make cupcake-style brownies instead by dividing batter equally among twelve muffin cups fitted with cupcake liners.

Substitute ½ cup walnut pieces for chocolate chips.

Note that this recipe creates a thin style of brownie (which bakes faster). Mama can't wait!

Top cooled Avocado Bolt Brownies with a rebooted portion of Frantic Vanilla Frosting (see recipe in this chapter).

Enjoy with a cold glass of "milk." One of my favorites is Silk Unsweet Vanilla Almondmilk with 0 grams net carbs per 1-cup serving.

ADDITIONAL RESOURCES

- For additional free resources, visit www.dirtylazyketo.com
- Want direct support from Stephanie? Join the private, limited-enrollment Premium DIRTY, LAZY, KETO support group for women only (subscription-based) "DIRTY, LAZY, KETO Premium Support Group by Stephanie Laska" at www.facebook.com/dirtylazyketo or www.facebook.com/becomesupporter/661359364046718/ through the Premium link at http://bit.ly/SupporterDLK.
- Listen to the author directly on the free podcast *DIRTY, LAZY, Girl* available wherever you listen to podcasts—links available at www.dirtylazyketo.com
- Get involved in the DIRTY, LAZY, KETO community:

  www.facebook.com/dirtylazyketo
  www.facebook.com/groups/DirtyLazyKeto
  www.youtube.com/c/DIRTYLAZYKETOStephanieLaska
  www.instagram.com/dirtylazyketo/
  www.instagram.com/140lost/
  www.pinterest.com/dirtylazyketo/
  www.twitter.com/140lost

RECIPE RESOURCES

CALCULATING RECIPE SERVING SIZES

The exact amount of a serving is clearly spelled out on nutrition labels, but not in recipes. Why is that? There are too many variables involved with cooking to provide an exact amount. The size of eggs you use or the size of your pans directly affects how much food is made. But let's not overcomplicate this. In the spirit of Lazy Keto, put away your food scales and measuring cups when estimating what portion to serve yourself. Follow this simple calculation instead:

Divide the recipe quantity by the *yield* to determine the serving size.

If a lasagna serves eight people and has 9 grams of net carbs per serving, cut your lasagna into eight even pieces and enjoy. Each piece of lasagna is a single serving, meaning each piece will contain 9 grams of net carbs. Easy-peasy!

GLOSSARY

As a courtesy, I've included a glossary of how I am using common keto vocabulary. (Keep in mind that my definitions might be different from what you have heard before.)

KETO AND KETO FACTIONS

Dirty Keto

Dirty Keto is eating whatever foods you choose within your macro goals or limits (which are different for everyone). Unfortunately, there are a lot of misconceptions about Dirty Keto. Critics are horrified about including junk food or processed meats into one's diet. They assume we survive *solely* on hot dogs and sugar-free Red Bull! *That's just not true.* Instead, Dirty Keto empowers you with more flexible options about what to eat. There is no judgment or strict rules about your lifestyle. You might "eat clean" during the work week but then live a little on the weekends. Foods aren't demonized either— artificial sweeteners and low-carb substitutes are fair game. Dirty Keto followers don't limit their food or beverage choices and might even be spotted drinking a Diet Coke (*oh, the horror!*).

DIRTY, LAZY, KETO

DIRTY, LAZY, KETO is not just a diet; it's a lifestyle. As a modern hybrid, it reaps the benefits of losing weight, but without limitations of food choices or the obligation of counting every macro. We eat foods that are higher in fat, moderate in protein, and lower in carbs, but allow for a little fun and flexibility. We are open to the idea of artificial sweeteners (Diet Coke or Splenda for example) and include packaged foods (protein bars, low-carb tortillas) in our meals. Dirty *and* Lazy Keto followers count only net carbs. I am the superhero of this category! I even coined the term. *Somebody make me a T-shirt!*

Keto

Keto is simply a shortened word for *ketogenic*.

Ketogenic diet

The ketogenic diet is a diet of foods high in fat, moderate in protein, and low in carbohydrates, with the goal of putting the body into ketosis.

Keto police

Keto police insist Strict Keto rules must be followed at all times! Though they don't wear a uniform, you can easily spot a member of the keto police by their social media posts that frequently ridicule others, arguing, "but THAT'S NOT KETO!" Keto police believe their purity and high standards make them superior; they constantly feel the need to educate and "correct" dissenting keto disciples.

Ketosis

Ketosis occurs when the body burns ketones from the liver as the main energy source (as opposed to using glucose as the energy source, derived from carbs). Ketosis is often an indicator (but not a requirement) of weight loss.

Lazy Keto

Lazy Keto followers only count their net carbs intake—not fat grams or protein intake. Lazy Keto does *not* mean unwilling to work hard for weight loss. This term refers to just counting a single macro in keto—the net carb—not a relaxed lifestyle or lack of energy. Not tracking doesn't mean overconsumption, though! Common sense is *always* used.

Strict Keto

Strict Keto adheres to a rigid and closely monitored ketogenic diet comsisting of no more than 20 grams of net carbohydrates per day. Followers insist on organic ingredients and avoid all processed foods. The keto prescription for weight loss never deviates: Calories distributed are distributed to a perfect ratio of 75 percent fat, 20 percent protein, and 5 percent carbohydrates.

If you are not sure what keto camp you fall into, try taking the free, short quiz I created on my website at www.dirtylazyketo.com/quiz/.

RELATED KETO TERMS

Calories

Calories are units of heat that food provides to the body. There are no "good" or "bad" calories. You've got to let this one go, people! A calorie is just an innocent unit of measurement, like a cup or a gallon. Our bodies *require* calories to survive. With DIRTY, LAZY, KETO, calories are not the focus (instead, net carbs are). The 1980s are over, my friends, and counting calories of low-fat foods is just as passé as leg warmers.

Carbohydrates/carbs

Carbohydrates, or carbs (for short), are sugars, starches, and fibers found in fruits, grains, vegetables, and milk products. Carbohydrates contain 4 calories per gram.

Chaffle

Chaffle started off as a portmanteau of "cheese waffles," but the term has since evolved to include a variety of recipes made with a waffle maker.

Fat

Fat is the densest form of energy, providing 9 calories per gram. The most obvious example of fat is oil (olive, coconut, sesame, canola, vegetable, and so on). Less clear examples of fats are dairy foods, nuts, avocados, and oily fish. Some fats have a better reputation than others (think about how the media portrays eggs, mayonnaise, Alfredo sauce, or chicken skin). No matter what the quality of the source, *fat is fat is fat.*

Fiber

Fiber is not digested by the body and is removed as waste. There are two types of fiber: soluble and insoluble. Fiber is a complex carbohydrate that does not raise blood sugar. *Fiber is your friend.*

Insoluble fiber

Insoluble fiber does *not* absorb water. Insoluble fiber moves through the intestine mostly intact, adding bulk to the stool and preventing constipation. Low-carb foods that contain notable amounts of insoluble fiber include blueberries, raspberries, strawberries, raw almonds, flaxseed, sesame seeds, walnuts, Brussels sprouts, cooked kale, and soybeans.

Keto flu

Keto flu is an avoidable set of symptoms (headache, lethargy, leg cramps) associated with dehydration, often experienced at the onset of the keto diet. Because the metabolic process of ketosis requires more water, increased hydration is required by the body.

Macronutrients/macros

Macronutrients, or macros, come in three packages: *carbohydrates*, *protein*, and *fat*. All macronutrients are obtained through foods in the diet, as the body cannot produce them. Each macro fulfills vital roles for your health. All macros contain calories but at different densities. Carbohydrates and proteins have 4 calories per gram, and fat has 9 calories per gram.

Net carbs

Net carbs are the unit of measurement tracked in DIRTY, LAZY, KETO. On a nutrition label, net carbs are calculated by subtracting all fiber and sugar alcohol grams from the listed amount of carbohydrates. Total carbs, minus fiber, minus sugar alcohol, equals net carbs. Net carbs are the leftover carbs in this mathematical equation.

Protein

Protein has 4 calories per gram. Proteins take longer to digest because they are long-chain amino acids. Protein is largely found in meats, dairy foods, eggs, legumes, nuts, and seafood.

Soluble fiber

Soluble fiber attracts water. When you eat foods high in soluble fiber, it turns to mush inside your body. Soluble fiber absorbs water quickly and helps to soften stool. It slows down your digestion and helps you to feel full. Examples of low-carb foods with notable amounts of soluble fiber include blackberries, strawberries, flaxseed, psyllium seed husks, artichokes, and soybeans.

Sugar alcohols

Sugar alcohols are reduced-calorie sweeteners. They do not contain alcohol! They are commonly used in sugar-free candy and low-carb desserts and are not digested by the body.

US/METRIC CONVERSION CHARTS

VOLUME CONVERSIONS

US VOLUME MEASURE	METRIC EQUIVALENT
⅛ teaspoon	0.5 milliliter
¼ teaspoon	1 milliliter
½ teaspoon	2 milliliters
1 teaspoon	5 milliliters
½ tablespoon	7 milliliters
1 tablespoon (3 teaspoons)	15 milliliters
2 tablespoons (1 fluid ounce)	30 milliliters
¼ cup (4 tablespoons)	60 milliliters
⅓ cup	90 milliliters
½ cup (4 fluid ounces)	125 milliliters
⅔ cup	160 milliliters
¾ cup (6 fluid ounces)	180 milliliters
1 cup (16 tablespoons)	250 milliliters
1 pint (2 cups)	500 milliliters
1 quart (4 cups)	1 liter (about)

WEIGHT CONVERSIONS

US VOLUME MEASURE	METRIC EQUIVALENT
½ ounce	15 grams
1 ounce	30 grams
2 ounces	60 grams
3 ounces	85 grams
¼ pound (4 ounces)	115 grams
½ pound (8 ounces)	225 grams
¾ pound (12 ounces)	340 grams
1 pound (16 ounces)	454 grams

OVEN TEMPERATURE CONVERSIONS

DEGREES FAHRENHEIT	DEGREES CELSIUS
200 degrees F	95 degrees C
250 degrees F	120 degrees C
275 degrees F	135 degrees C
300 degrees F	150 degrees C
325 degrees F	160 degrees C
350 degrees F	180 degrees C
375 degrees F	190 degrees C
400 degrees F	205 degrees C
425 degrees F	220 degrees C
450 degrees F	230 degrees C

BAKING PAN SIZES

AMERICAN	METRIC
8 × 1½ inch round baking pan	20 × 4 cm cake tin
9 × 1½ inch round baking pan	23 × 3.5 cm cake tin
11 × 7 × 1½ inch baking pan	28 × 18 × 4 cm baking tin
13 × 9 × 2 inch baking pan	30 × 20 × 5 cm baking tin
2 quart rectangular baking dish	30 × 20 × 3 cm baking tin
15 × 10 × 2 inch baking pan	30 × 25 × 2 cm baking tin (Swiss roll tin)
9 inch pie plate	22 × 4 or 23 × 4 cm pie plate
7 or 8 inch springform pan	18 or 20 cm springform or loose bottom cake tin
9 × 5 × 3 inch loaf pan	23 × 13 × 7 cm or 2 lb narrow loaf or pate tin
1½ quart casserole	1.5 liter casserole
2 quart casserole	2 liter casserole

INDEX

ABOUT THE AUTHORS

USA TODAY bestselling author and creator of DIRTY, LAZY, KETO, Stephanie Laska doesn't just talk the talk; she *walks the walk*. She is one of the few keto authors that has successfully lost half of her body weight (140 pounds!) and maintained that weight loss for eight years *and counting*.

Want the "full story" on how you, too, can lose weight for good? Check out the blockbuster *DIRTY, LAZY, KETO®: Get Started Losing Weight While Breaking the Rules* (St. Martin's Essentials, 2020), the guidebook that started an international trend to help hundreds of thousands of fans lose weight in a revolutionary new way.

Expect humor, honesty, and inspiration from your DLK girlfriend, Stephanie Laska. Her mission is to help as many people as possible fight obesity *one carb at a time*! She fights back against the shame, blame, and judgment surrounding obesity with DIRTY, LAZY, KETO.

Stephanie's honest sass and fresh approach to the keto diet break all the traditional rules of dieting. You might have caught her cooking debut with Al Roker on NBC's *Today* show. Her story and image have been celebrated in articles or images shared by Fox News, *Parade*, *US News & World Report*, *New York Post*, *Reader's Digest*, *Yahoo! News*, *First for Women*, *Woman's World*, *Muscle & Fitness: Hers*, *Keto for You*, runDisney, and *Costco Connection*. She has run a dozen marathons—most notably the New York City Marathon as a sponsored athlete from PowerBar. Not bad for a girl who ran her first mile (as in ever!) close to age forty.

Alongside her coauthor and husband, William Laska, Stephanie has created more support tools: *The DIRTY, LAZY, KETO® Cookbook: Bend the Rules to Lose the Weight!* (Simon & Schuster, 2020), *The DIRTY, LAZY, KETO® Dirt Cheap Cookbook* (Simon & Schuster, 2020), and *DIRTY, LAZY, KETO® Fast Food Guide: 10 Carbs or Less* (Amazon, 2018). Stephanie also hosts a free weekly podcast, *DIRTY, LAZY, Girl*, available for listening on YouTube, Apple Podcasts, or wherever you currently listen to podcasts.

Stephanie and Bill reside in sunny California. When they aren't talking about their third child (DIRTY, LAZY, KETO), the Laskas enjoy running, traveling "on the cheap," and shopping at thrift stores.